THE
FOUR
GOSPELS

Mark J Musser Books
2018

The Four Gospels Devotional

Copyright © 2018 Mark J. Musser

Cover art: Image ID: 78776646 (L); Image ID: 41838873 (M)

First printing 2018

Printed in the United States of America

Unless otherwise indicated, all Scripture quotations are taken from *The Holy Bible*, New Living Translation, copyright © 1996, 2004, 2007, 2013, 2015 by Tyndale House Foundation. Used by permission of Tyndale House Publishers, Inc., Carol Stream, Illinois 60188. All rights reserved.

Trade paperback: ISBN: 9781790182091

Special Thanks To:

God for guiding my steps and for my wife
and son who put up with my missteps.

"A BOOK THAT TACKLES THE CONTEMPORARY AND THE CONTROVERSIAL WITH TRUTH AND GRACE."

The Hills of Vincere Ridge

Life is anything but easy for fourteen year-old Jason Collins. Adopted and raised by a same-sex couple, his standard school day consists of lingering stares, not-so-subtle whispers, and outright bullying. His only escape, hours of quiet solitude working on his golf swing. Then one weekend, hearing the words of Jesus--*Come to me all of you who are weary and carry heavy burdens, and I will give you rest*--Jason comes, trusting those words to prove true.

Life, however, gets infinitely more difficult. While his moms struggle with his decision to trust Christ, a publicity seeking pastor manipulates the teen into petitioning for new legal guardians, setting off a firestorm of protests, picketing, and media baiting.

Enter TJ Lanter, a former professional golfer still working to overcome his own tragic past. Together, the two fight to use their shared loved of golf to create a bond that enables both to see through their pain and discover that Jesus does indeed embrace the weary and give them rest.

LET THE NEXT 100 DAYS BE
THE FIRST 100 DAYS OF THE REST OF YOUR LIFE!

The First 100 Days of the Rest of Your Life

Life is not a sprint. It is not even a marathon. No, life is a Tough-Mudder, Iron-Man, and Spartan Race all rolled into one! Perhaps, in the middle of this race, you have found yourself exhausted, overwhelmed, depleted, and defeated. If so, it's time for a restart. Grab hold of this devotional and let the next 100 days be the first 100 days of the rest of your life.

George Muller wrote, "The vigor of our spiritual life will be in exact proportion to the place held by the Bible in our life and thoughts." A.W. Tozer once commented, "Nothing less than a whole Bible can make a whole Christian."

Some devotionals offer you only a Scripture or two followed by a short blurb and a pithy quote. If you are looking for spiritual nourishment, that would be nothing more than a light snack. True spiritual sustenance requires much more.

If you want a "full meal," check out The First Hundred Days of the Rest of Your Life. This transformation-driven devotional will provide you with a portion of Scripture to read, a handful of questions to think through, suggested prayers to offer up, and action steps to apply God's Word.

Find this devotional on Amazon today!

THE COMPANION DEVOTIONAL TO *THE FOUR GOSPELS* !

The Letters of Paul -- Devotional

Just like Paul's letters, this devotional does not add any water to the Gospel. On this 90-day journey, you will follow along with Paul as he teaches total surrender not agreeable assent, Christ-likeness over fitting in, and living by the standards of God's Word over the suggestions of the culture.

Some devotionals use hardly any Scripture at all or tout building faith in just five minutes a day. That is NOT this devotional. Using Mark Musser's tried and tested S-C-R-I-P-T method, each devotional has six sections. Every day begins with START HERE where you will read a humorous or interesting intro. What follows is the CONSIDER section which will provide a brief overview of the biblical chapter focused on for the day. After that comes READ, where that day's chapter is studied. Once the chapter has been read through, you will head to the INVEST portion which usually contains five to seven questions to get you thinking about what was read and how it affects daily life. Next comes PRAY. In this area, suggestions are offered on what should be prayed about that particular day. Finally, TRAINING offers practical steps to take during the day to help apply the Word to life.

Find this devotional on Amazon today!

FOLLOW THE S-C-R-I-P-T

Searching for a swiveling TV stand, I found one online that looked fantastic. However, when I received it, the instructions left much to be desired. The box itself was printed with many "helpful" tips like: "Please carefully put on this product if placing a heavy article like TV. Please should not allow heavy article fall down." And "please should be carefully especially for children."

Huh? I can only assume the writer was using the new Common Core curriculum!

Anyway, I hope this instructional page will be slightly clearer for you! Thanks for investing in this devotional which will take you through the letters of Paul. We'll be traveling through eighty-nine chapters in the Bible! That's impressive.

Before we start this journey, however, allow me to share how each devotion is set up. You will find that they all contain six sections, each starting with a letter that spells the word S-C-R-I-P-T.

Every devotion begins with **START HERE** where you will read a humorous or interesting intro. What follows is the **CONSIDER** section which will provide a brief overview of the biblical chapter you focus on for the day. After that comes **READ,** where you will read through that day's chapter. Once you have studied the chapter, you will head to the **INVEST** portion which usually contains five to seven questions to get you thinking about what you read and how it affects your daily life.

Nearing the end, you will find **PRAY.** In this area, you will find suggestions on what you should be praying about that particular day. Finally, **TRAINING** offers practical steps to take during the day to help apply the Word to your life.

Be aware. This devotional does not add any water to the Gospel. Instead, it will boldly challenge you to strive after the standards, requirements, and expectations of God's Word. This devotional teaches total surrender not agreeable assent, and Christ-likeness over fitting in. I want this book to point you to a holy God that desires to guide your life, not tag along with what you are doing.

Are you ready to grab hold of a vision to follow Christ, not culture. I hope so because that is the purpose of this book. If you are ready to let God change you so you can change the world, then let's get started!

MATTHEW 1

START HERE
I am completely perfect.

Well, maybe not completely perfect. I do have four tiny flaws: 1. I lack humility. B. I am inconsistent. 4. I can't count.

You see, we all have flaws. But flaws or not, God can still use us to change the world.

CONSIDER
As we start our read through the Gospels, don't rush through all the names you will encounter in chapter 1. Be sure to read carefully, giving thought to each name listed. Note that *all* the names listed up through Zerubbabel are from the Old Testament, and *all* had their share of issues. In fact, a few people listed had some major issues! Yet, each one is a part of Jesus' lineage.

Today, if you are a child of God, then are you also part of Jesus' lineage. Like many of those you will encounter in chapter 1, you are flawed. But don't let that keep you from being used mightily by the Lord.

As you read, consider if you are letting past mistakes and present flaws keep you from making a difference for Christ.

READ: MATTHEW 1

INVEST
In verse 19, Joseph is described as what type of man?

How do you think people would describe you?

Listed in Jesus' lineage are Abraham, Isaac, and Jacob. All of them had trouble with lying. Tamar prostituted herself; David was an adulterer and a murderer; Solomon put his pleasure before the Lord; Rehoboam was immature, and the list continues. Knowing this, how can Jesus' lineage encourage you to serve the Lord in spite of past mistakes and present flaws?

Joseph sincerely wanted to honor God—even if it meant marrying a woman who seemed to be pregnant by another man. How sincere is your desire to serve the Lord?

In what areas might you struggle with serving?

What can you do this week to serve the Lord?

PRAY
- Thank God for loving you in spite of your past mistakes and present flaws
- Confess, if necessary, using your past as an excuse not to serve the Lord in the present
- Ask the Lord to forgive and restore you
- Ask the Lord to use you to make an amazing difference in this world

TRAINING
- Make sure to review the last question in INVEST
- List the ways you can make a difference through service this week—consider how you can serve your family, your coworkers, your neighbors, and beyond
- Contact your pastor or the church office and ask what serving opportunities are available

MATTHEW 2

START HERE
Santa lives at the North Pole;
Jesus is everywhere.

Santa rides in a sleigh;
Jesus rides on the wind and walks on the water.

Santa comes but once a year;
Jesus is an ever-present help.

Santa fills your stockings with goodies;
Jesus supplies all your needs.

You have to stand in line to see Santa;
Jesus is as close as the mention of His name.

Santa lets you sit on his lap;
Jesus lets you rest in His arms.

Santa doesn't know your name, all he can say is "Hi, little boy or girl, what's your name?"

Jesus knew our names before we did. Not only does He know our name, He knows our history and future and He even how many hairs are on our heads.

Santa has a belly like a bowl full of jelly;
Jesus has a heart full of love.

Santa says, "You better not cry."
Jesus says, "Cast all your cares on me for I care for you.

Santa's little helpers make toys;
Jesus makes new life, mends wounded hearts, repairs broken homes and builds mansions.

While Santa puts gifts under your tree,
Jesus became our gift and died on the tree.[1]

CONSIDER

It is usually known as the "Christmas Story," but the events of chapter 2 are much more than that. In today's Scripture, you will encounter three types of people. First, you will meet King Herod. He is the man in charge and doesn't want that fact to change. His bottom sits firmly on the throne, and no one else's bum is allowed to make new cheek marks on the cushion.

Second, there are the religious leaders. They clearly understand that the Messiah will come and even know that He will be born in backwater Bethlehem, yet they seem utterly indifferent to the news that the Christ's blessed coming may have actually happened! Those leaders are too comfortable—they have the most authority, the best clothes, and the nicest life as "the respected ones." Why upset the apple cart? Let the baby stay in Bethlehem.

Finally, we will meet the Magi—wise men from the East. They have forsaken all else to follow a star, no matter where it leads. They are diligently seeking and will do all they can to find the new-born King to bestow upon Him all that He deserves.

As you read, consider which of the three types you are.

READ: MATTHEW 2

INVEST

Herod wanted to sit on the throne and make all the decisions. In what ways are you like Him?

The religious leaders were very comfortable with the status quo and not interested in having Jesus come along and upset the way things were. In what ways are you like those leaders?

Frankly, many of us are a good mix of Herod and the religious leaders—living a comfortable life where we make all the decisions about where we will spend our time, what entertainment we will choose, how money will be spent, etc. Where do you struggle with these things?

The wise men were on a dangerous journey, crossing hostile areas not knowing if there would be water, food, or safety. Nevertheless, they left everything familiar behind to seek after Christ. In what ways are you like the wise men?

In what areas do you need to work so that you can be more like them?

PRAY
- Thank God for the people in your life that are examples of surrendering to, and sacrificing for, Jesus Christ
- Confess, if necessary, being too much like Herod and the religious leaders and not enough like the wise men
- Ask the Lord to mold you into a person who diligently seeks after Jesus Christ
- Ask the Lord to work on the areas that are too much like Herod and the religious leaders

TRAINING
Think through these questions:
- Are you like Herod? You say you want to meet with Christ. And, yes, you are willing to worship Him, but you still plan on making all the decisions. The throne of your heart belongs to you
- Are you like the religious leaders? Without a doubt, you could surely meet with Christ today through His Word, through prayer, through church, and through conversation with other believers, but life is busy and really not all that bad right now. You're comfortable, so, eh, maybe later
- Are you like the wise men? Maybe the pursuit of Christ seems foolish to those around you, but you don't care. There is nothing more important to you. You desire to pursue Christ. Regardless of how difficult the journey may be, you will give your best—even if that means constant sacrifice

For the sake of a world that desperately needs to see Christ, I hope you will choose to be like the wise men. I pray you will choose to pursue Christlikeness with all that you are for all of your days.

MATTHEW 3

START HERE

A man woke up in the morning genuinely repentant after a bitter fight with his wife the previous night. He noticed with dismay the crate of beer bottles that had caused the fight. He took it outside and started smashing the empty bottles one by one onto the wall. He smashed the first bottle swearing, "You are the reason I fight with my wife!" He smashed the second bottle, "You are the reason I don't treat my children as I should!" He smashed the third bottle, "You are the reason I don't have a decent job!" When he took the fourth bottle, he realized that it was still sealed and full. "You stand aside, I know you were not involved."[2]

Yes, it's one thing to say you are sorry, but quite another to live out being sorry.

CONSIDER

Repentance—to turn away.

As noted above, it is easy to say, "Lord, I want to follow You. Please forgive me and help me to live for Your pleasure." Living out these words, however, is not so easy.

We say we want to follow Jesus but go off and choose our own path. We say we want to live for Jesus but then live for our own pleasure. We ask the Lord to forgive our sins but never actually turn away from them—it's just the same thing over and over and over again.

As you read, consider if you are really living out your faith or just saying that you are.

READ: MATTHEW 3

INVEST

What does it mean to repent?

How are you doing at *living* like you follow Christ?

According to today's reading, what happens to trees (i.e. people) who produce bad fruit?

What does John the Baptist say in verse 8?

Have you been proving with your life that you are a follower of Christ?

What's going well? What needs work?

PRAY
- Thank God for proving His love for you by sending Jesus to die on the cross for your sins
- Confess, if necessary, talking the talk but not walking the walk
- Ask the Lord to forgive you where necessary
- Ask the Lord to help you turn away from sin and to live fully for Him

TRAINING
- Review your thoughts, actions, attitudes, words, interactions, and entertainment choices over the past two weeks
- What may need to be truly repented of, so you can live fully for Christ?

MATTHEW 4

START HERE

John and Sarah were struggling to make ends meet after building their dream home. One day they went shopping, the husband went to the men's clothing section and his wife to the women's section. A little later Sarah came back with a five hundred dollar dress she had just bought! "How could you do this?!" John was aghast.

"I was outside the store looking at the dress in the window, and then I found myself trying it on," Sarah explained. "It was like Satan was whispering in my ear, 'You look fabulous in that dress. Buy it!'"

"Well," John retorted, "You know how I deal with that kind of temptation. I say what Jesus said in the Bible, 'Get behind me, Satan!'"

"I did that!" Sarah answered. "But then he said, 'It looks fabulous from back here, too!'"[4]

CONSIDER

Temptation. We all battle it. And, let's face it, at one time or another we have fallen victim to it. The bad news is that we will *never* be free of these temptations—for even Jesus was tempted. The good news, however, is that we don't need to keep losing battles. Through Christ, we can have victory as He did!

As we begin to experience more and more victory over temptation, then the words of Paul to Timothy can come true: *If you keep yourself pure, you will be a special utensil for honorable use. Your life will be clean, and you will be ready for the Master to use you for every good work.*[3]

As you read, consider if you are overcoming temptation in Christ's power, or if temptation is still the victor much too often.

READ: MATTHEW 4

INVEST

Jesus was tempted three times, and three times He used Scripture to combat

Satan. With that in mind, do you have Scripture memorized to fight off Satan's lies and lures?

How are you doing in your own battle with temptation?

How can you do better? What tools can you employ during times of temptation?

According to verses 20 and 22, how long did it take for the disciples to respond to Jesus' call?

Staying with the theme of temptation—when we are tempted but hear Jesus calling us away from alluring situations or thoughts, how quickly should we respond?

What happens when you don't heed Jesus' voice "at once" and allow the devil to get a foothold?

How can understanding the need to flee temptation immediately help you better deal with it in the future?

PRAY
- Thank Jesus that He is there to be your refuge in times of temptation
- Confess, if necessary, falling to temptation too often
- Ask the Lord to enable you to run to Him in the midst of struggles, trials, and temptations
- Ask the Lord to mold you into a disciple that responds at once to His voice

TRAINING
To best fight off temptation, use the following seven steps:

- First, pray for the Lord to lead you from temptation. Praying with others is also a great way to help, as well as asking trusted friends to pray for your strength to overcome specific sins
- Second, understand your weak areas. The devil knows them, so you better! Don't put yourself in situations and places that can easily cause temptation
- Third, learn to recognize temptation. The more you study Scripture and attune yourself to Truth, the easier it will be to detect Satan's lies and the world's lures
- Fourth, take preventative action. If you know certain situations will bring you into temptation (going to a bar, going online by yourself, watching certain movies, being around the wrong people, etc.), then take preventative action to avoid those things
- Fifth, memorize Scripture. The Bible calls itself "the sword of the Spirit." It is our offensive weapon in our battle with the devil
- Sixth, be sure to rest. We are more susceptible to temptation when we are exhausted. Rest is essential for our spirituality, and we must be extra vigilant when tired, asking the Lord for the strength needed to resist temptation
- Seventh, remember there is always a way of escape. God never allows us to be tempted beyond what we can take but always provides us with a way out[5]

MATTHEW 5

START HERE

After an exceptionally long and boring sermon, the congregation filed out of the church, not saying a word to the pastor. After a while, a man shook the pastor's hand and said, "Pastor, that sermon reminded me of the peace and love of God!"

The pastor was ecstatic. "No one has ever said anything like that about one of my sermons before! Tell me, how did it remind you of the peace and love of God?"

"Well," said the man, "it reminded me of the peace of God because it passed all human understanding, and it reminded me of the love of God because it endured forever!"[6]

Thankfully, for Jesus' listeners, the Sermon on the Mount would have only taken about twenty to twenty-five minutes to preach. (Now, for someone to tell my pastor that!)

CONSIDER

The Sermon on the Mount begins.

In His first recorded sermon, Jesus spends Matthew 5-7 basically saying, "This is what you think you know, but now let Me tell you how it really is." He is breaking down old misconceptions and misunderstandings in preparation for building up His new church. He is calling for us to quit following the culture and the crowd so that we can follow Him, and He is challenging us to set aside all else so we can all grab hold of Him.

As you read, consider who or what you follow. Is it the culture, the crowd, or Christ?

READ: MATTHEW 5

INVEST

What is Jesus saying in verses 13-16?

How are you doing at being salt and light in your home, your neighborhood, your classroom or workspace, etc.?

What is going well? What needs work?

In verses 21-48, Jesus repeatedly declares, "You have heard it said…but I tell you…" What is Jesus attempting to do in this section of His sermon?

How are you doing with verses 44-48?

What is going well? What needs work?

Who or what do you most follow? The culture's ideas, the crowd's pressure, or Christ's truth?

PRAY
- Thank Jesus for the truth of His Word
- Confess, if necessary, flowing along with the culture or the crowd over following Christ
- Ask God to give you opportunities to be salt and light to those around you
- Ask God to help you love as He loves

TRAINING
- Begin praying today and ask God to use you as salt and light in the world
- Start walking around your neighborhood praying for your neighbors. Ask God to open your eyes to see where you can make a difference right on your own street
- Learn your spiritual gifts. Seek to understand how God has shaped you to serve Him. Ask your pastor if your church has a class on spiritual gifts.
- Think through this question: What passions has God placed on your

heart?

- Understand the desires God has placed on your heart and get involved in a local church or ministry that needs people with those passions
- Make a list of three to five friends, relatives, associates, and neighbors who don't know Jesus as their Lord and Savior. Place that list where you will see it often and pray for those people whenever you see the list. Ask the Lord to open those individuals to the Gospel, and pray for opportunities to share God's Word with them

MATTHEW 6

START HERE

There's a story about a severely overweight woman who hired a personal trainer to help her lose weight. This trainer placed the woman in front of a full-length mirror and had her look at herself. Embarrassed by her appearance, she could barely peek for more than a few seconds. Meanwhile, the trainer took a permanent marker and created an outline of a slimmer figure on the mirror. He then told the woman, "If you do what you must, you will look like this."

Each day, the woman met with her trainer, worked out, exercised, and watched what she ate. Discipline became the name of the game. At the end of each week, she would stand in front of that mirror again, and, each week, she still did not fit into the lines. Yet, she was moving closer.

Finally, after more than twenty months of diligent exercise, discipline, and healthy choices, she stepped in front of that mirror and fit that outline exactly.

Understand that this story is not about the woman becoming a size 00 supermodel. No, it is about a woman disciplining herself to make consistently healthy choices. Likewise, this story is not meant to be an analogy about you becoming the next Billy Graham or Mother Teresa. No, it is about you making the choices necessary to better seek the Kingdom of God.

It might seem a daunting task to make the Kingdom number one in your life, but every journey begins with a single step. When we discipline ourselves by watching what we put into our hearts and minds, by doing the hard work of Bible study, by investing in prayer, and by faithfully surrounding ourselves with a group of like-minded believers, we begin to deepen and mature, to take on the character of Christ, and to seek after what He seeks after.

CONSIDER

As the Sermon on the Mount unfolds, Jesus continues to drive the people toward a new way of thinking and living. Yesterday, in chapter 5, there were many "You have heard it said…but I tell you…" as the Lord worked to change how we relate to God and others. In chapter 6, He is going to dig deeper into those things, while also adding a new component—money and possessions.

As you read, consider if you have God's perspective, or the world's perspective, on who He is, how to treat others, and the purpose of money and possessions.

READ: MATTHEW 6

INVEST
In verses 1-8, Jesus talks about doing things out of a desire to honor God versus a desire to show off. In your own life, do you speak and act for God's glory or for your own?

What might need to change?

According to verses 14-15, why must we forgive others and not hold grudges?

In verses 19-24, what does Jesus say about possessions and money?

If your heart is where your treasure is, then where is your heart?

Do you hold God's perspective on possessions and money (it's all His), or do you have the culture's view of these things (it's mine, all mine)?

What does verse 33 say?

If you spent every day seeking first the Kingdom, would your life look much different than it does right now? Why or why not?

PRAY
- Thank God for taking care of all your needs
- Confess, if necessary, having the world's perspective over God's perspective
- Ask the Lord to enable you to seek first His Kingdom every single day

- Ask the Lord to help you live for His glory and not your own

TRAINING
- Spend some time in prayer. Surrender everything over to the Lord. Give Him free rein in you and over your life and possessions
- Ask Him where, and with what, He wants you to sacrifice time, treasure, and talents for His glory and the benefit of a lost world
- Are you saving up for something? A car, vacation, new home, super big screen TV, etc.? Consider taking that savings and investing it in a ministry, a missions' trip, or missionaries already stationed in the field
- How much time each week do you watch TV? Commit to cutting that in half for one month. Use the extra time to get involved in your neighbors' lives, volunteer at a local ministry or at your church, etc. You might find that after the month is up that your life is much more fulfilling with less television and more world changing
- Join a small group at your church. (If your church does not have small groups, join a small group at a friend's church.) Spend time with other believers, asking God how you can be used to make a difference in people's lives

MATTHEW 7

START HERE

A little boy was talking with the girl next door, "I don't really have any money, so I am not sure what to get my mom for Mother's Day."

"Well," the girl started, "You could promise to keep your room clean, go to bed right when she tells you, come as soon as she calls you, brush your teeth without being asked, and stop fighting with your sister."

"No," the little boy replied, "I need something more practical."

There is a lot of that little boy in all of us. We often wish to give God something in return for all He has done for us. Of course, what the Lord truly wants is obedience, while we are always looking to give "something more practical."

CONSIDER

In chapter 7, Jesus wraps up His first recorded sermon. He began in chapter 5 by seeking to establish a new normal—"You have heard it said…but I tell you…" This means coming to Christ involves a new way of thinking. No longer do we follow the culture or the crowd. Instead, we follow Him.

In chapter 6, Jesus makes it clear that we are not only to think in a new way, but we are to relate to God and others in a new way as well. We must put God first, see all of our possessions as His, and love all others (even enemies). As we head into chapter 7, Jesus prepares to conclude by informing all who will listen that this whole thing only works when we fully obey. There are no half-measures. It is either all in or all out.

As you read, consider if you are all in or if you are trying to have one foot in the world and one foot in the Kingdom.

READ: MATTHEW 7

INVEST

Jesus knows that, instead of searching our own hearts and minds to determine if we are all in or not, we will look at others and focus on how they fall short. What does the Lord say about this in verses 3-5?

Are you guilty of focusing on the faults of others more than your own? If so, what can you do about this?

What is Jesus saying in verses 15-20?

If people looked at the fruit of your actions, attitudes, words, choices, etc., what would they say about that fruit?

Like the people in verses 21-23, we can come to the Lord with, "Hey, I read the Bible, pray, and have gone on missions' trips. Aren't you pleased with me, Lord?" But what does Jesus say about this in verse 21?

On a scale of one to ten (with one being "poorly" and ten being "I am incredible!") rate how active you are in fulfilling God's will for your life:

If you did not give yourself a ten, what needs work?

In verses 24-27, what is the difference between the person who listened and obeyed and the person who just listened?

Which one are you?

PRAY
- Thank God for the people in your life who are great examples of living obediently
- Confess, if necessary, not listening and obeying the Lord as you should
- Ask the Lord to help you to listen and obey
- Ask the Lord to guide you deeper into His will and further into a world that desperately needs to hear the Good News

TRAINING

- Has God laid something on your heart that you've continually dismissed because it seemed too big or too hard? If so, now is the time to revisit it. Begin praying about it and let the Lord lead you
- Schedule a meeting with your pastor. Ask about the most significant needs in the church and see if God may want to use you to fill that need
- Pray this dangerous prayer: "Father, I can't be a world changer from my comfort zone, so lead me out of my comfort zone into a world that desperately needs you."
- Gather your family together and come up with a list of things you can do together to serve the Lord
- Remember to keep praying for the three to five unsaved friends, relatives, neighbors, coworkers, classmates, etc. on your prayer card

MATTHEW 8

START HERE
Many parents today think it improper to discipline their children, but one prop engine pilot found an effective way to handle his children's misbehavior. "Since I'm a pilot, one method that I have found very effective is for me to just take the child for a short flight during which I say nothing and give the child the opportunity to reflect on his or her behavior."

"I don't know whether it's the steady vibration from the engines, soaring over beautiful scenery at five hundred feet, or just the time away from any distractions such as TV, video games, computer, iPod, etc. Either way, my kids usually calm down and stop misbehaving after our flight together. I just wait for them to promise good behavior, then I let them back inside the plane and safely land."

CONSIDER
Care and power. Those things don't seem to go together very often. The caring and compassionate often eschew power and position, so they can invest in helping others. Meanwhile, the powerful and authoritative tend to focus on goals, tasks, and details, so they can advance a cause or build a career. Rarely, however, can we find someone who is genuinely caring and truly powerful all at once.

In chapter 8, though, we find Jesus showing the depths of His love and care as well as the extent of His majesty and power. Yet, to experience these dual characteristics of Christ, we must be willing to forsake all else and commit to following Him wherever He leads.

As you read, consider that to experience all the compassion and care that Jesus offers, we must be willing to submit to His power and authority.

READ: MATTHEW 8

INVEST
In Matthew 8:1-4, Jesus touches a leper (an unthinkable thing to do in His day). Why is Jesus touching an "untouchable" such good news for us?

Why is it comforting to know that no matter how deep the stain of your sins, Jesus is willing to hug you, hold you, and forgive you?

How does Jesus display His power in verses 23-32?

Where do you need Jesus' power to go to work in your life?

What does Jesus say about commitment in verses 18-22?

How committed to Jesus are you? What parts of your life are not submitted to Him?

PRAY
- Thank Jesus for being both caring and powerful, compassionate and authoritative
- Confess, if necessary, wanting the compassion of Jesus without submitting to His authority
- Ask the Lord to work on your weak areas
- Ask the Lord to fill you with a desire to humbly serve Him

TRAINING
- Evaluate how you have been spending your time over the last few weeks. Understand that if Jesus is the reason for everything, you cannot be content with free time spent solely for self
- Continually remind yourself that this world is not your home and that everything in the world that you hold so dear will pass away
- Consider how much of your life is surrendered to the Lord. Is it one hundred percent? If not, what parts have not been surrendered yet?

MATTHEW 9

START HERE

A young man named James was walking along a steep cliff when he accidentally got too close to the edge and fell. On the way down he grabbed a branch, which temporarily stopped his fall. He looked down and to his horror saw that the canyon fell straight down for more than a thousand feet.

He couldn't hang onto the branch forever, and there was no way for him to climb up the steep wall of the cliff, so James began yelling for help, hoping that someone passing by would hear him and lower a rope or something. "HELP! HELP! Is anyone up there? HELP!"

Suddenly, as if by some miracle, he heard a voice from above, "I can see you, James. I am the Lord, and I have come to rescue you."

"Yes, God, please help me!" James shouted, his grip on the branch getting weaker and weaker.

"I will, My child," the Lord answered back. "I just need you to do one thing."

"I'll do anything, Lord. Just tell me what to do."

"Let go of the branch and have faith in me."

"Huh?"

"I said, let go of the branch. Just trust Me. Let go."

"HELP! HELP! Is anyone else up there?!?"[7]

CONSIDER

The word most often translated as "faith" in the New Testament comes from a Greek root word that means "a pledge to live out what you believe." We see this in action quite often in chapter 9. A tax collector gives up his profession to follow an itinerant preacher, friends carry a paralyzed man to see life change, a debilitated woman pushes through a crowd (breaking Jewish law in doing so) to find restoration, blind men feel their way into a home to receive sight, and a man defies the hatred of his fellow religious leaders in order to experience his daughter raised from the dead. All of this because of faith—

belief put into action.

As you read, consider how well you are living out what you believe.

READ: MATTHEW 9

INVEST

What happened to the lame friend because others believed Jesus could do something for him?

Who are you bringing to Jesus through your life of faith?

Matthew sacrificed a lucrative career to follow Jesus. What have you sacrificed to give Christ your all?

Several religious leaders mocked, questioned, and doubted Jesus (and that was on a good day!) Another religious leader, however, had faith enough to defy his counterparts and run to Jesus for a miracle. How do you react when those around you refuse to believe? Do you still stand for Christ?

The bleeding woman was considered "unclean" because of her condition. This meant she could not be around others, let alone touch them. Yet, she defied convention and grabbed hold of Jesus. Are you willing to challenge cultural expectations and convention to grab hold of Jesus and live for Him?

What can you do this week to work the harvest?

PRAY
- Thank the Lord for those who willingly worked in your life and shared Christ with you
- Confess, if necessary, being more of a "secret believer" instead of a fully invested, active person of faith

- Ask the Lord to grow your faith and help you to live out what you say you believe
- Pray to the Lord of harvest, beseeching Him to send workers out into the fields

TRAINING
- Spend some time with the last question in the INVEST section
- Think and pray through what you can do in your home, your neighborhood, your church, your workplace or school, etc.
- Gather with others and brainstorm together

MATTHEW 10

START HERE

Back around the year 2000, I was living six hours from Houston, Texas and decided I would visit a friend who lived there. Pulling directions off the internet (no smartphones with GPS back then), I headed on my way.

I easily made it into east Texas without a hitch...then the problems started. First, one of the nastiest thunderstorms I ever experienced rumbled through. Within minutes of passing a "Welcome to Texas" road sign, I was in a deluge. Some welcome! As if that wasn't bad enough, it seemed all of East Texas was undergoing road construction. Detours took me well off my internet directions.

Not having a cell phone at that time, I found a gas station, pulled up to the phone booth, and dialed my friend's number. After five or six rings, all I got was the answering machine. Great! Not knowing what else to do, I did what any man would rather not do. I asked for directions.

Later, lost again, I stopped at another gas station to use yet another pay phone. (Here is where the story goes from "bad" to "Heaven help me.") The pay phone was actually out in the middle of the parking lot with no cover. (Remember the deluge?) That meant standing in a downpour while dialing. Voicemail.

Meanwhile, the rain is soaking me literally to the bone, and my useless internet directions were disintegrating into a soggy mess. Thoroughly frustrated, I went to get back in my car. (Here's where the story goes from "Heaven help me" to "Lord, take me, please!") Pulling on the door handle, I suddenly realized that I locked my keys in the car, and the car was running!

By the time I was able to get my car door jimmied open, every part of my being was wet. Thoroughly dejected, I went into the gas station one last time and actually sat on the floor of the men's room, under the hand dryer, repeatedly hitting the "on" button trying to dry off.

Now, I have a simple rule that I live by when it comes to trips. It goes something like this: *When you find yourself on the floor of a gas station men's room underneath a hand dryer, that is the point in the trip when you should decide, "I'm going to pack it in."*

Pack it in is what I did, and I dragged my soggy body back home. Dead tired upon arriving, I still did one more thing before crawling mercifully into bed. I sent my amigo a "specially worded" email liberally detailing how he let me down by not being at his phone.

The next morning, I read my friend's reply. He had been caught in the same deluge while mowing someone's lawn and sought cover, away from his cell phone, until the storm passed. Oh yes, and one more thing, he also wrote that the gas station I was last at sat less than a mile from his home!

If I had only held on a little longer, if I had just trusted my friend a little more, my trip would have been a whole lot different. Let's not allow that to be said in our relationship with Jesus. Let's hold on as long as it takes. Let's trust Jesus with all that we are. If we do, our trip on this journey called life will be a whole lot different.

CONSIDER
In case you were unaware, life is not easy.

Through the first nine chapters of Matthew, we've seen Jesus doing some awesome and amazing things through faith. But a life of faith doesn't mean all will be rainbows and butterflies. In chapter 10, Jesus will make it clear that faith makes life better, but it doesn't make it easier. In fact, living out your faith might even make things more difficult! Regardless, we need to stand firm no matter what—through the good, the bad, and the car rides to Texas.

READ: MATTHEW 10

INVEST
Many blessings come through faith in Christ, yet Jesus makes it plain that "life in Me won't just be a joyride." According to chapter 10, how can faith in Christ actually mean difficulty and trials?

How do you handle things when life gets difficult?

How can verses 29-31 encourage you when things get tough?

What is Jesus saying in verses 37-39?

Do you have anything in your life that takes first place from God?

If so, what should you do with these things?

PRAY
- Thank God for being with you through the good, the bad, and the ugly
- Confess, if necessary, following God when things are good but complaining and giving up when things are tough
- Ask the Lord to shore up your faith
- If you are going through difficulties right now, hand them over to the Lord

TRAINING
- Keeping God first is the best way to maintain the proper perspective when life gets tough
- That being the case, review the "F-I-R-S-T Philosophy" by asking yourself if God first in your Finances, Interests, Relationships, Schedule, and Time
- Isolate the areas where God has been pushed out of His rightful first position and make changes as necessary

MATTHEW 11

START HERE

After hearing a sermon about the need to share the Gospel, Gary committed to praying each day, "Lord, if you want me to witness to someone today, please give me a sign." A couple days later, he found himself on a bus when a big, burly man sat next to him. The bus was nearly empty, but this guy sat next to our praying friend. "Lord, is this the sign?" Gary whispered to himself.

A few minutes later, as Gary anxiously waited for his stop so he could get off the bus, the burly man burst into tears and began to weep uncontrollably. "Lord, is this the sign?" Gary whispered again.

Suddenly, the man cried out with a loud voice, "I need to be saved. I'm a lost sinner, and I need the Lord. Won't somebody tell me how to be saved?!?"

Gary immediately bowed his head and prayed again, "Lord, is this the sign?"[8]

Well, we don't need "signs" from the Lord about evangelism, for His Word is clear. We *should* be sharing the Gospel as often as we can.

CONSIDER

There will always be people who doubt, deny, reject, and outright hate the Gospel message, however; there will also be those ready to embrace Christ. We must be willing to deal with the first group of people if we want to give the second group a chance to be transformed by the Savior.

As you read, consider how you handle it when people are antithetical to the Gospel. Do you shrink back or continue forward?

READ: MATTHEW 11

INVEST

The people of Jesus' day refused to see Him and His followers for who they were – messengers of hope and life. How is that like much of America today?

What are you doing to be a messenger of hope and life for Christ?

Reading about Tyre and Sidon (as well as Sodom), you would think everyone in those places was irredeemable. Yet, Jesus said if He had been at work there, those people would have repented! Who do you know today that seems irredeemable?

What do verses 21-24 tell us could happen if you allow Jesus to work through you in their lives?

What is Jesus saying in verses 28-30?

Have you experienced this change that Christ can bring?

How can you help others experience this change?

PRAY
- Thank Jesus for taking your burdens and providing you with peace and life
- Confess, if necessary, shrinking back from sharing the Gospel because you fear rejection, mocking, hate, etc.
- Ask the Lord to work through you to change lives
- Pray specifically for the ones you wrote down under the third question in the INVEST section

TRAINING
- In the devotional on Matthew 5, you were instructed to make a list of five friends, relatives, co-workers, classmates, and/or neighbors who you know are not saved. If you have not already done so, do so now
- Commit to praying over that list every day, asking the Lord to work in their hearts and to give you a chance to make a difference in their lives

MATTHEW 12

START HERE

The following are actual excuses written on insurance forms after a car accident.

- Coming home I drove into the wrong house and collided with a tree I don't have
- I thought my window was down, but I found it was up when I put my head through it
- I collided with a stationary truck coming the other way
- The guy was all over the road. I had to swerve a number of times before I hit him
- I pulled away from the side of the road, glanced at my mother-in-law, and headed over the embankment
- In an attempt to kill a fly, I drove into a telephone pole
- I had been driving for forty years when I fell asleep at the wheel and had an accident
- I was on the way to the doctor with rear end trouble when my universal joint gave way causing me to have an accident
- To avoid hitting the bumper of the car in front, I struck a pedestrian
- My car was legally parked as it backed into another vehicle
- An invisible car came out of nowhere, struck my car, and vanished
- The pedestrian had no idea which way to run as I ran over him
- I saw a slow moving, sad faced old gentleman as he bounced off the roof of my car
- The indirect cause of the accident was a little guy in a small car with a big mouth[9]

Excuses. Excuses. We don't just use them when trying to get out of trouble. We also use them when trying to get out of sharing our faith!

CONSIDER

The doubt, confusion, rejection, and hatred that filled chapter 11 is going to be ramped up in chapter 12. Undaunted, though, Jesus continues to advance the Kingdom in the face of all the adversity because He understands what is at stake. His message is the only thing that can change the world.

As you read, consider if you are willing to face any challenge or struggle to ensure that all those around you can experience the hope of the Gospel.

READ: MATTHEW 12

INVEST

What is the good news of verse 21?

Why is it vital to remember this truth when life gets hard, or you feel misunderstood/rejected because of your faith in Christ?

How do verses 33-37 serve to give you pause when you might be tempted to be careless with your words and actions?

In what areas do you need to better guard your words and deeds?

Throughout this chapter, Jesus dealt with hate, doubt, rejection, and more, yet He was not deterred. How about you? Do you tend to get quiet or step back when people challenge or reject your faith and message?

PRAY
- Thank Jesus for being the hope of the world
- Confess, if necessary, shrinking back from sharing this hope because of a fear of rejection, scorn, or hatred
- Ask the Lord to embolden you to fearlessly share His truth
- Ask the Lord to help you guard your words and deeds that you might honor Him in all that you say and do

TRAINING
- Review the language you use, the attitudes you exude, the actions you show, and the behaviors you consistently repeat. Do they all reflect Christ? What may need to change? (Don't be afraid to ask others to evaluate you in these areas)
- Review the media you ingest. What movies and TV shows do you watch? What music do you listen to? What websites are you frequenting? Are these all things that Christ Himself would spend time

with?

- Review how you react when wronged, when your children blow it, when your spouse irritates you, when your favorite sports' team is losing, etc. Does your attitude need adjustment in any of these areas?
- Review how you communicate and show love to family, friends, neighbors, coworkers, classmates, etc. How you express and demonstrate love is a good indicator of how well people will see Jesus in you

MATTHEW 13

START HERE

A duck hunter took his new hunting retriever out on its first hunt anxious to test him out. Sure enough, within a couple minutes, the hunter hit a duck, and it fell into the lake. The dog walked across the water, picked up the duck, and brought it back to his master.

The hunter's neighbor, who was in a nearby duck blind, was flabbergasted! Before he could say anything, though, another shot was fired, and another duck dropped into the lake. Once again, the dog walked across the water to fetch the duck.

The neighbor couldn't contain himself any longer. "I've never seen anything like this in my entire life!"

"Neither can I," the hunter responded, "This dumb dog can't swim!"

Yes, it is true. From time to time, we humans can be a bit dense. Sadly, when it comes to matters of faith, that denseness increases geometrically!

CONSIDER

Understanding the nature of the Kingdom of God is vitally important. Because of this, Jesus continually taught what it is, what it isn't, and what is required to gain citizenship in it. As chapter 13 unfolds, in spite of all that is swirling around Him—doubt, fear, rejection, anger, subversive plots—Jesus continues this instruction. The question is: Were the people listening?

As you read, consider how earnestly you seek to understand what it means to be part of God's Kingdom.

READ: MATTHEW 13

INVEST

As Jesus explains the Parable of the Seeds, what does He say about those who represent the second and third seeds?

People who are like the second seed do not have deep roots and so soon fall away when life gets hard, or there is pushback to their faith. How can a robust devotional life help keep you from becoming like this seed?

Those who are like the third seed are easily distracted by the things of the world. Without a focus on Kingdom pursuits, their faith is choked and withered by a lack of time and attention to it. How can you avoid this in your own life?

What will help you be more like the people of the fourth seed?

Based on verses 30, 41, and 50, why should you be diligent in sharing your faith and the good news of God's Kingdom?

What is the message of verses 44-46?

The Bible says that Jesus told these two short parables to show us what the Kingdom of Heaven is like. In both stories, the individuals were willing to give up everything to get something of great value. Their friends and family probably thought they were crazy, but the first guy knew what was in the field and the pearl merchant recognized a true treasure when he saw it. Likewise, perhaps those around you will think you are crazy to be sold out for Christ, but this is what the Kingdom of Heaven is supposed to be about—giving up everything to get it! What about you? Do you know that Jesus is worth it? And, if so, how are you living that out?

Where are you not all in for the Gospel? What parts of you are not entirely surrendered?

PRAY
- Thank Jesus for giving up His whole life for you because He thought you were truly worth it
- Confess, if necessary, living more like seed two and three instead of the fourth seed

34

- Ask the Lord to help you be someone who produces much fruit
- Commit to the Lord. Tell Him you are ready to be all in regardless of what others think or say about it

TRAINING

- In His excellent book, *Not a Fan*, Kyle Idleman writes, "Fans will be careful not to get carried away. Followers understand that following Jesus is a pursuit that may cost them everything, but it is the best investment they could make. Followers will do crazy things for love. Fans want to play it safe...but Jesus will settle for nothing less than to be the great love and pursuit of your life."[10] With this quote in mind, think through what you have not yet surrendered to Jesus
- Spend some time thinking and praying about what you could do for Jesus this week that perhaps your friends or family might think is crazy

MATTHEW 14

START HERE
A British Parliament Committee noted in 1878 that Edison's light bulb was "good enough for our Transatlantic friends... but unworthy of the attention of practical or scientific men."

In 1911, Ferdinand Foch, a French general and Allied Commander during World War I, said, "Airplanes are interesting scientific toys, but they are of no military value."

In 1902, the *New York Times* called the automobile impractical, complaining that the price of cars "will never be sufficiently low to make them as widely popular as were bicycles."

In 1928, Joseph Schenck, President of United Artists, seemed confident about one thing: talking pictures were a fad. He told the *New York Times* that "talking doesn't belong in pictures." Though he conceded that sound effects could be useful, he felt that dialogue was overrated. "I don't think people will want talking pictures long."

In 1977, the founder of Digital Equipment Corporation said, "There is no reason anyone would want a computer in their home." Not to be outdone, Thomas Watson, the president of IBM, stated, "I think there is a world market for maybe five computers."

Looking back at history, we can see that doubt and lack of belief were sorely misplaced on more than one occasion. Looking back at our own lives, I hope we all recognize that doubt and lack of belief in God are always sorely misplaced.

CONSIDER
Faith. We've seen a lot of it during our journey through the first half of Matthew. However, in chapter 14, if you are hoping to see more, you will be severely disappointed! For when it comes to faith, the only thing the twelve disciples show is a stunning lack of it!

Now, it would be easy for us to condemn them for their unbelief in Someone who had done so much already, but we need to ask ourselves how different from them we really are. As you read, consider how many times you doubt

God's goodness and wonder if the Lord will really pull through for you.

READ: MATTHEW 14

INVEST
How many baskets of leftovers were there?

What lesson do you think each disciple learned as his basket of leftovers got heavier and heavier?

What did Jesus say to Peter in verse 31?

How often do you think He has said similar words to you?

Is there something in your life that is causing you to doubt right now?

What should you do with these doubts?

PRAY
- Thank God for always being there to see you through each and every situation that comes crashing into your life
- Confess, if necessary, being like Peter and the other disciples all too often
- Ask the Lord to deepen and mature your faith
- Give to the Lord any doubts or fears you might be having right now

TRAINING
- You can imagine each of the twelve disciples, with their basket in tow, collecting all the leftovers. As they pick up piece after piece, weighing down their basket more and more, a realization hopefully struck them: "Wow! Jesus can be trusted. He not only provides; He exceedingly provides."

- Similarly, spend some time filling a basket of your own. List all the many ways that the Lord has blessed you, taken care of you, held you through a situation, etc.
- Keep adding to your basket until it is overflowing, and you have been filled anew with the understanding that Jesus not only provides; He exceedingly provides

MATTHEW 15

START HERE
Heading to the office this morning, I noticed a woman driving ten miles over the speed limit with her face up to her rear view mirror, putting on eyeliner! The next thing you know, she was halfway in my lane, still putting on her makeup.

I don't scare easily. But she so jarred me, I dropped my electric shaver, which knocked the donut out of my other hand. In all the confusion of trying to straighten out the car using my knees against the steering wheel, it knocked my cell phone away from my ear which fell into the coffee between my legs, ruined the phone, soaked my trousers, and disconnected an important call. All because of that crazy woman driver![11]

Yes, it is all too easy to focus on another's issues to avoid looking at any of our own.

CONSIDER
It's often surprising when people we think should understand something, don't, and those we think won't get it, do. In chapter 15, the Pharisees (who know the Old Testament better than literally everyone else on the planet) and the disciples (who spend their every waking moment with Jesus) are squarely in the "don't get it" camp. Meanwhile, a gentile woman, with virtually no understanding of the Scriptures, and minimal contact with Christ, totally gets it!

As you read, consider the fact that we should never pre-judge anyone. Those we firmly believe are far from Christ might be closer than we think!

READ: MATTHEW 15

INVEST
What is Jesus saying in verse 11 and verses 17-20?

How is your own heart looking right now? What, if anything, needs to be confessed and cleaned out?

How does this chapter show that the Pharisees simply aren't getting it?

In chapter 14, Jesus fed thousands of people, yet what happens when He talks to the disciples about feeding a smaller crowd?

It is easy to come down on the disciples, but how often has God taken care of you and then you seem to "forget" all about it the next time something difficult occurs?

Jesus was in a Gentile area ministering to Gentile people, so why do you think He spoke to the woman the way He did in verses 21-28?

The Lord is always working to test and to deepen our faith. Where is He currently doing this in your life?

As we discussed under CONSIDER, everything points to the Pharisees and the disciples embracing Christ and to the Gentile woman rejecting Him, yet the opposite happened. How does this show that we cannot pre-judge where a person's heart is?

Have you been guilty of misjudging people?

What can you do to rid your mind of preconceived ideas whenever you encounter someone new?

PRAY
- Thank the Lord for the understanding He has given you
- Confess, if necessary, doubting God in spite of all the many things He has already done for you
- Ask the Lord to remind you of His goodness the next time you are in a difficult circumstance
- Ask the Lord to keep you from judging someone's heart

TRAINING

Do you struggle with pre-judging people? Here are a few things that can help you curb that tendency:

- Monitor your thoughts. When you meet someone, watch coming to conclusions too quickly. Engage in conversation, working to keep your mind a blank slate

- Look for the positive. There is almost always something positive you can find in someone. If you focus on looking for it, you will find it!

- Avoid stereotyping. Take each person as you find him or her. Get to know people individually without lumping them into a group

- Focus on your own life. It's easy to look at others and find every flaw. When you are tempted to do that, remind yourself that you are far from perfect

- Remember how it feels to be judged. We all want to be accepted based on who we are, not based on who someone *thinks* we are[12]

MATTHEW 16

START HERE
I used to think that I was indecisive, but now I'm not too sure.

Indecisiveness is called by many names—waffling, flip-flopping, yo-yoing, imitating my wife when I ask where she wants to go out to eat, and more. We humans are undoubtedly fickle creatures, changing our minds more often than squirrels change direction in the middle of the road...and we know what happens to them!

When it comes to our relationship with God, it is very much the same. One minute we are firm in our faith, the next we are squishier than my midsection. One minute we are on fire for Jesus, the next we could sink the Titanic if it hit us.

When will we all learn to simply trust and believe no matter what? Here's an idea. Let's answer that question with: *Today*!

CONSIDER
As we have seen through the first fifteen chapters of Matthew, the Gospel has been forcefully advancing. Jesus is preaching and teaching, healing and changing lives. However, the Pharisees (who know the Scriptures best) refuse to believe the Scriptures point to Him. Meanwhile, the disciples (who spend every waking moment with Jesus) seem more confused than clear and more filled with doubt than filled with faith.

In chapter 16, though, some of that confusion and doubt begins to ebb away (at least temporarily!) Peter proclaims that Jesus is the Messiah, the Son of the living God. For about five minutes, all is right with the world...until Peter opens his mouth again! After Jesus lays out a hard truth, the big fisherman takes Jesus by the hand, leads Him away from the others, and rebukes the Lord Almighty! In the Greek, it reads that Peter "severely censured" Jesus. In Italian, it reads, "Whataya nuts!?!"

Of course, it is easy to come down on Peter for his sonic-speed, one hundred and eighty-degree turn, but we are often no different. On Sunday morning, we sing praises to the King of Kings, then on Sunday afternoon, we receive some bad news and vehemently complain to the Lord, wondering what in the world He is doing.

As you read, consider how like Peter we all really are.

READ: MATTHEW 16

INVEST

In chapters 14 and 15, Jesus miraculously fed thousands of people, yet what are the disciples complaining about in verse 7 of this chapter?

How does Jesus respond in verses 8-11?

How often has the Lord taken care of you and your needs, yet you still doubt His goodness during difficult times?

At long last, one of the disciples (Peter) seems to break through the clouds of doubt and confusion and recognize Jesus for who He is (in verse 16). However, what do we see Peter doing in verse 22?

Why do you think that Jesus calls Peter "Satan" in verse 23?

It is scary to think that when we reject Jesus' will and authority, we are just like Satan. How can reminding yourself of this truth help you the next time you are about to question what God is up to?

In verse 24, Jesus says that to be His follower, we must deny ourselves, pick up the cross, and follow Him. What does it mean to do this?

Where do you need work with these three things?

PRAY
- Thank Jesus for being Lord, Messiah, and Savior
- Confess, if necessary, praising God one minute and complaining to

Him the next

- Ask the Lord to help you always follow His will and submit to His authority
- Ask the Lord for the strength to deny yourself, pick up your cross, and follow

TRAINING

To deny self, pick up your cross, and faithfully follow Christ, you will need to recognize a few key things:

- You are *not* in charge anymore. Jesus is in charge. He is the boss, and you are the worker
- Life is *not* about comfort and pleasure. Kingdom living means trading in temporary comforts and pleasures for the lasting joy of serving Christ
- You *cannot* do this your way in your strength. You must, moment by moment, stay connected to Christ so that His Spirit can fill you with the strength to be and to do all that God is calling you to be and to do

MATTHEW 17

START HERE

Not too long ago, while reading through the news online, I came across the story of a "bridezilla" who went above and beyond to make sure she was the center of attention on her wedding day.

With her two better-looking sisters set to be bridesmaids, this bride-to-be chose dresses that would make the two look "washed out and slightly ill." She, then, also started preparing "special slimming" smoothies for her none-the-wiser sisters that they drank each morning for several months leading up to the wedding.

However, these "slimming" drinks were actually filled with mega-weight gain protein powder! To make it all believable, she bought a large container of weight loss shake powder, emptied the contents, and added the weight-gain. Her sisters remained clueless the entire time.

As the wedding day approached, the sisters' waists were thickening rapidly, much to the pleasure of bridezilla. She states, "The day went off without a hitch, and everyone had a great time. I never thought for a moment on my wedding day that I wasn't the center of attention or the most important person in the room…and now, when I look back on my wedding photos – as I do often as we've got them displayed around the house – I sometimes feel a twinge of guilt that I'm standing there glowing and gorgeous in my bridal gown, and my sisters are looking washed out and chubby. But mostly I feel happy."[13]

That newlywed's level of self-centeredness is quite stunning, though we all tend to slide into selfishness from time to time. This is what makes Jesus all the more amazing. No matter what He was going through, His focus was always on glorifying the Father and blessing the world.

CONSIDER

In yesterday's devotional reading, we saw that Jesus, for the first time, clearly announced His impending death to the disciples. Today, he will do so once more. Incredibly, even though He is fully aware of the terrible punishment that lies before Him, the Lord busily continues revealing His glory, healing lives, and teaching the masses.

It would be quite understandable if Jesus started to focus a bit more inwardly as He prepares for the torturous task ahead, but that is not what He does. As you read, consider if you make life more about God and others or more about yourself. And, when life is hard, consider if you tend to dwell on "your issues" or if you continue living out God's plan for your life.

READ: MATTHEW 17

INVEST

Moses and Elijah enter the scene to speak with Jesus, presumably to comfort and direct Him as He prepares to suffer and die. Who comforts you when you are struggling?

Are you quick to share when difficult things are occurring in your life, or do you keep those things to yourself?

Why is it essential that you reach out to others who can comfort you and offer prayer support?

Through Jesus' experience with Moses and Elijah, three of the disciples were able to get a glimpse of the Lord in His glory. What situations in your life have enabled you to really see Jesus at work?

What does Jesus tell the disciples in verses 20-21?

How deep is your faith? What areas might need some work?

God often uses difficulties and struggles to develop our faith and trust. How have you experienced this in your own life?

PRAY
- Thank God for being with you in the tough times and for using those times to heighten and mature your faith

- Confess, if necessary, not sharing your struggles with others and/or not allowing the Lord to use difficult times to help you grow
- Ask the Lord to provide trusted friends with whom you can share your hurts and struggles
- Ask the Lord to use any difficult situation in your life to expand your faith

TRAINING
- If you don't already have one, find a prayer partner
- Share with this person any difficulties or struggles you are experiencing
- Ask this person to share hurts and burdens with you so that you can stand in the gap through prayer

MATTHEW 18

START HERE
From an unknown source comes an article titled, "How to Be Miserable." It says, "Think about yourself. Talk about yourself. Use 'I' as often as possible. Mirror yourself continually in the opinion of others. Listen greedily to what people say about you. Expect to be appreciated. Be suspicious. Be jealous and envious. Be sensitive to slights. Never forgive a criticism. Trust nobody but yourself. Insist on consideration and respect. Demand agreement with your own views on everything. Sulk if people are not grateful to you for favors shown them. Never forget a service you have rendered. Shirk your duties if you can. Do as little as possible for others."[14]

I don't think this is how God intended us to live. Do you?

CONSIDER
How we interact with others is important. Life cannot just be about us and what we want. (Bummer, I know.) Let's face it. Most of us are much more inwardly focused than outwardly focused. Because this is the case, in Matthew 18, Jesus is going to teach on the need to think about our interactions with others—how our choices may affect their lives, what we do that causes temptations in others, why we must offer forgiveness, the proper way to correct and restore others, and more.

As you read, consider how you are doing at those things.

READ: MATTHEW 18

INVEST
According to verse 6, what is better in God's eyes than causing others to be tempted?

It is incredible to think that Jesus basically says, "Listen, if there's a choice between you causing someone to be tempted or being held underwater by a heavy object until you drown, I would prefer you were held underwater!" Why do you think Jesus uses such stark language in verse 6 (and verses 7-9)?

What might need to be "cut off" (i.e., removed) from your life to help you better follow Christ?

When someone offends you, do you follow the steps outlined in verses 15-20 instead of gossiping, complaining to others, refusing to communicate, etc.?

In the parable of the unforgiving debtor, the first servant owed the king the equivalent of 375 *tons* of silver. (That's over 177.5 million dollars!) This was truly an unpayable debt, yet the king gracious forgave it. Meanwhile, someone owed the forgiven servant the equivalent of ten thousand dollars, and he refused to forgive the debt. How did the king react to this news?

In this parable, God is the king. We have sinned against Him so many times, it is, frankly, an incalculable amount! Yet, we are graciously forgiven whenever we plead for His mercy. The fact is that no one could come close to sinning against us as much as we have sinned against God. Why is this important to remember whenever someone offends you?

What do verses 34-35 say will happen with us when we refuse to forgive others as graciously as we have been forgiven by God?

To whom do you need to offer forgiveness?

PRAY
- Thank the Lord for forgiving you times without measure
- Confess, if necessary, not offering the same forgiveness to others
- Ask the Lord to help you relate to others in a way that pleases Him
- Ask the Lord to enable you to forgive as easily and as graciously as He does

TRAINING
A study by the Mayo Clinic found that letting go of grudges and offering forgiveness leads to:
- Healthier relationships

- Improved mental health
- Less anxiety, stress, and hostility
- Lower blood pressure
- Fewer symptoms of depression
- A stronger immune system
- Improved heart health
- Improved self-esteem

Meanwhile, holding onto grudges and refusing to forgive causes:
- Anger and bitterness to enter into every relationship and new experience
- An inability to enjoy the present because you are so wrapped up in a past wrong
- Depression and anxiousness
- Lost times of enriching connectedness with others[15]

Which do you prefer?

MATTHEW 19

START HERE

The story is told of a prosperous, young investment banker who was driving a new BMW sedan on a mountain road during a snow storm. As he veered around one sharp turn, he lost control and began sliding off the road toward a steep cliff. At the last moment, he unbuckled his seat belt, flung open his door, and leaped from the car, which then plummeted to the bottom of the ravine and burst into a ball of flames. Although he had escaped with his life, the man suffered a ghastly injury. Somehow his arm had been caught near the hinge of the door as he jumped and had been torn off at the shoulder.

A passing trucker saw the accident in his rearview mirror, pulled his rig to a halt, and ran back to see if he could help. When he arrived at the scene, he found the banker standing at the roadside, looking down at the BMW burning in the ravine below. Incredibly, the banker was oblivious to his injury and moaned, "My BMW! My new BMW!"

The trucker pointed at the banker's shoulder and said, "You've got bigger problems than that car. We've got to find your arm. Maybe the surgeons can sew it back on!'"

The banker looked where his arm had been, paused a moment, and groaned, "Oh no! My Rolex! My new Rolex!"[16]

Our young banker friend has his priorities a bit backward. How about you? Are your priorities in the proper order?

CONSIDER

As we saw in the last chapter, God takes seriously how we relate to, and interact with, others. In chapter 19, Jesus continues on with the theme of relationships—Marriage is foundational, children (who were considered just above property in Bible times) are precious, but, most importantly, God must be our number one relationship. As foundational as marriage is, and as precious as children are, they do not compare to our relationship with the Lord.

Some selfishly put themselves first. Others, thinking they are selfless, sacrifice much to put family first. But if time with God is cast aside to do that, then, as St. Augustine once stated, you have "disordered loves." As you read, consider who or what you have been putting first.

READ: MATTHEW 19

INVEST

In verses 4-6 and 9, why does Jesus say a husband and wife should not divorce?

In verse 14, what does Jesus say to the disciples when they try to keep the little children from coming to Him?

How do these two situations in verses 1-15 show that Jesus cares about our relationships with friends and family?

As important as those relationships are, the most important relationship we have is with the Lord. Jesus works to show this through the story of the rich young man. What did Jesus say the man needed to do "to be perfect" in verse 21?

How did this young man react to Jesus' words?

The young man wanted a to-do list. Jesus, however, wanted a relationship. In essence, Christ told the man, "Set everything aside and come be with Me, spend time with Me, and go where I go." The young man was unwilling to set aside everything else to put Jesus first. How about you? Are you willing to sacrifice time with others, with hobbies, or with whatever/whoever else so you can grow, deepen, and mature in your relationship with Jesus? Explain:

PRAY
- Thank Jesus for putting you first and dying in your place for your sins
- Confess, if necessary, not putting, or keeping, Christ first in your relationships
- Ask the Lord to help you have great relationships with family, friends, neighbors, coworkers, classmates, etc.
- Ask the Lord to devote you to keeping Him first above everyone and everything else

TRAINING

In Matthew 10, we briefly discussed what it looks like to keep God F-I-R-S-T. That is, making sure God is first in Finances, Interests, Relationships, Schedule, and Time. Today, let's look at this more intently:

- When it comes to finances, does God get the first ten percent of your income? Do you set aside or delay purchasing certain wants in order make sure you can tithe?
- Is God first in your interests? When you have free time, what is the first thing you go to? The garage? The internet? The phone? The mall? The golf course? The TV? Or do you go to prayer, to God's Word, to a Christian book, to a service project?
- In regard to relationships, is God your primary one? Do you make sure to invest in this relationship daily, or does the Lord get set aside for other relationships or other pursuits?
- When it comes to your schedules and your time, where does God rate? When you have a scheduling conflict between the things of this world and the things of God, which one wins? If there is a picnic or the kids have a soccer game on Sunday morning, what choice do you make? Is God first in all scheduling conflicts?

MATTHEW 20

START HERE

A young woman asked for an appointment with her pastor to talk with him about a besetting sin about which she was worried. "Pastor," she started, "I have become aware of a sin in my life which I cannot control. Every time I am at church, I begin to look around at the other women, and I realize that I am the prettiest one in the whole congregation. None of the others can compare with my beauty. What can I do about this sin?"

"Well, Mary," the pastor replied. "What you are describing is not a sin. It's a mistake!"[17]

They say pride is the only disease that makes everyone else sick but the one who has it. If that is the case, let's all pray that we are not making those around us ill.

CONSIDER

Pride, like sin, is a word with "I" right smack dab in the middle of it.
"I deserve this."
"I should be first."
"I have my rights.
"I want to…"
I, I, I.

The Bible talks much about pride because it is the most significant barrier to living life for Christ. Life in Christ requires humility, surrender, and sacrifice. Pride, however, prefers ego, exaltation, and gain. As you read, consider if "I" or "God" is at the center of your life.

READ: MATTHEW 20

INVEST

In the parable of the vineyard workers, what did the first workers think they deserved?

Do you tend to think you "deserve" stuff? Why do you think that is?

How did John and James show pride in verses 20-22?

In verse 24, what did their fellow disciples think about this?

How did Jesus respond to them all in verses 25-28?

In verse 28, Jesus states that He is prepared to sacrifice His life for others. How does this contrast with the attitudes of James, John, and the other disciples?

Who wins most frequently on an average day for you: "I" or "Christ"?

If you are struggling with pride and "I" issues, what must you do?

PRAY
- Thank Jesus for exemplifying humility, surrender, and sacrifice
- Confess, if necessary, there being too much "I" in you and not enough "Christ"
- Ask the Lord to forgive your pride
- Ask the Lord to fill you with Himself—His humility, selflessness, and love

TRAINING
- If you struggle with pride, strive to focus more on the greatness of God
- Remind yourself of Acts 17:28, *For in him we live and move and exist.* Understand that your abilities all come from the Lord. You can't even bat an eyebrow or move your pinky if God did not give you the ability
- Relinquish any "rights" you think you have. The only thing we rightfully deserve is an all-expenses paid trip to Hell, yet Jesus paid the price so we could enter Heaven
- Endeavor to be grateful and thankful. Literally count your blessings. Live a life of thankfulness

MATTHEW 21

START HERE
Dr. Harry Ironside was once convicted about his lack of humility. A friend recommended as a remedy that he march through the streets of Chicago wearing a sandwich board, shouting the Scripture verses on the board for all to hear. Dr. Ironside agreed to this venture.

When he returned home later that day, he removed the board, proudly telling everyone, "I'll bet there's not another man in town who would do that."[18]

William Temple wrote, "Humility does not mean thinking less of yourself than of other people, nor does it mean having a low opinion of your own gifts. It means freedom from thinking about yourself one way or the other at all."[19]

May we all seek that kind of humility.

CONSIDER
Sin and pride, both words with "I" right smack dab in the center, are on full display in chapter 21. Both are contrasted by a solitary figure humbly riding a donkey's colt into Jerusalem. Fascinating how the Savior of the world is filled with humility, while lost sinners are filled with pride!

As you read, consider if you are more like Jesus or more like the crowd. Are you following John the Baptist's lead from John 3:30—*"Jesus must become more and more, and I must become less and less"*?

READ: MATTHEW 21

INVEST
The cursing of the fig tree was an acted out analogy of people who look good, yet their lives produce no fruit because they are inwardly focused. Do you tend to be overly concerned by how you appear to the world but not so concerned about producing fruit for the Kingdom?

We see a similar analogy in verses 28-32. One son wants to look good but not be good, while one doesn't look good but ends up being good. Today, it is easy to get caught up in "playing church" while not being the church. With that in mind, do you need to repent of not living out the gospel?

The evil tenants pridefully wanted to be their own boss. Do you ever struggle with rejecting God's will and authority, so you can do what you want?

In verse 43, Jesus states that the Kingdom is taken from the unrepentant and prideful and given to those who desire to produce fruit pleasing to God. How are you doing at producing this type of fruit?

What is going well? What needs work?

PRAY
- Thank God for the opportunities He gives to repent and try again
- Confess, if necessary, any prideful thoughts, words, or actions
- Give your life over to the Lord in humble submission
- Ask the Lord to enable you to produce amazing fruit for His kingdom

TRAINING
- For the next few moments, become a fruit inspector and assess samples of your actions, attitudes, words, and thoughts over the past week or so. How Christ-like have they been?
- Has your life been complying with the Word of God to ensure your optimal spiritual health?
- When it comes to the standards set forth by Christ and His Word, where are you doing well? Where have you been falling short?
- Take the above questions to someone who knows you well. Ask this person to answer these questions about you—allow him or her to do some inspecting

MATTHEW 22

START HERE

In *U.S. Naval Institute Proceedings*, the magazine of the Naval Institute, Frank Koch illustrates the importance of obeying the Laws of the Lighthouse. He writes that two battleships assigned to the training squadron had been at sea on maneuvers in heavy weather for several days. The visibility was poor with patchy fog, so the captain remained on the bridge keeping an eye on all activities.

Shortly after dark, the lookout on the wing reported, "Light, bearing on the starboard bow."

"Is it steady or moving astern?" The captain called out.

The lookout replied, "Steady, Captain," which meant they were on a dangerous collision course with that ship.

The captain then called to the signalman, "Signal that ship: 'We are on a collision course, advise you change course twenty degrees.'"

Back came the signal, "Advisable for you to change course twenty degrees."

The captain said, "Send: 'I'm a captain, change course twenty degrees.'"

"I'm a seaman second class," came the reply. "You had better change course twenty degrees."

By that time the captain was furious. He spat out, "Send: 'I'm a battleship. Change course twenty degrees.'"

Back came the flashing light, "I'm a lighthouse."

They changed course.

In our lives, God is the lighthouse. Are you ready to change course when He commands?

CONSIDER

Authority is an integral part of life. As children, we grow up with authority figures—parents, coaches, teachers, etc.—who give us practice at listening, heeding, and obeying. Once grown, authority figures still fill our lives—supervisors, bosses, small group leaders, pastors, and more. Learning to obey these figures gives us practice submitting to God's authority. Indeed, the more we practice obedience in earthly relationships, the less we will question, doubt, or reject God's authority.

As you read, consider if you practice obedience (even when you don't want to) to help you better submit to the Lord.

READ: MATTHEW 22

INVEST
In Bible times, to refuse an invitation from the king was tantamount to treason. With that in mind, in verse 7, how did the king react when many of the invitees refused to come?

In Bible times, it was considered the height of disrespect to not wear the proper attire to a special occasion. In essence, it was saying, "I don't care enough about this to do what is expected or right." With that in mind, in verse 13, what did the king do to the fellow who failed to dress appropriately?

How do you think God likes it when you disrespect or disobey the authority figures He has placed in your life?

Where might you need work submitting to, and honoring, the authority figures God has placed in your life?

The religious leaders hated Jesus because He threatened to upset the order of things and become the new authority figure for the people. For this reason, they were continually scheming to trap or trick Jesus into saying or doing something for which He could be arrested. What things do you tend to do to make sure that you are the one who keeps making the decisions for your life?

Where do you need work submitting to, and honoring, God's authority?

PRAY

- Thank God for the authority figures He has placed in your life
- Confess, if necessary, not honoring those authority figures or God's authority in your life
- Ask the Lord to fill you with a desire to obey those in authority over you
- Ask the Lord to fill you with a desire to obey His authority over your life

TRAINING

- Review your interactions with the authority figures in your life over the past few weeks. Which interactions were positive? Which ones might need some work?
- Review your choices over the past few weeks. How many of them were made with God's will in mind?

MATTHEW 23

START HERE
Have to sit through a boring lecture in your near future? Try these tips to stay entertained:

- Contradict everything the speaker says with "That's what *you* think!"
- When the lecturer asks a question, raise your hand. If called on, point to someone else and say, "He knows." Pick a different person each time
- Buy a doll. Leave the doll in your chair, along with your notebook and pen. Say that you have an important meeting to go to, and the doll will be taking notes for you
- Bring a typewriter. Use it to take notes
- Bring a fully-stocked picnic basket. Explain that you didn't have time to eat breakfast
- Bring a fishing rod. Try to catch things off the speaker's lectern
- Raise your hand and ask when the movie is going to start
- Bring a flash camera. Take pictures every few minutes, using a very bright flash
- Run across the room, tag someone, yell "You're it!" then race back to your seat
- If any of the above gets you in trouble, mumble loudly about how much you hate Sharpie's[20]

Okay, I *really* don't recommend any of those. During lectures, it's usually a good idea to simply listen and learn.

CONSIDER
Most of us aren't the biggest fans of lectures. If I had the choice between sitting through a thirty minute PowerPoint presentation or having a spider burrow into my ear, I would have to think about it before deciding!

Well, in Matthew 23, Jesus is going to give the lecture of all lectures. And, believe me, by the time it's over the religious leaders would be wishing they chose the spider! In one of the harshest homilies of all time, Jesus lays into the hypocritical, self-righteous Pharisees. If the phrase "tear them a new one" existed back then, it would have been used after this lecture!

As you read, don't think about how awful the religious leaders were. Instead, dare to ask yourself, "Am I like them in any way?"

READ: MATTHEW 23

INVEST

The lecture Jesus gives here is often referred to as the "Seven Woes" because seven times Jesus states "Woe to you" (in the King James translation). These "woes" are necessary, Jesus says, because of verse 5. What does the first sentence of verse 5 state?

Have you been guilty of doing things in an effort to look good to others?

What does Jesus say in verse 12?

What does He mean?

In verses 23-24, Jesus says the religious leaders work hard to make sure they look very pious while lacking any real desire to follow the Lord. Have you been guilty of desiring to look good over desiring God?

In verses 25-28, Jesus makes it plain that no matter how good we make the outside look, God still sees what's going on inside. With that in mind, where do your insides need work?

In spite of all their faults and sins, what does Jesus say in verse 37?

In spite of the peoples' sin, pride, and rejection of Him, Jesus stands with His arms open wide. How does this encourage you in the midst of your struggles with sin and/or pride?

PRAY
- Thank Jesus for His unconditional love that is always ready to envelop

you
- Confess, if necessary, being a little too much like the religious leaders
- Ask the Lord to work on any "inside" issue that you are currently struggling with
- Ask the Lord to break down any pride you might have

TRAINING
- If you have been guilty of spending a great deal of time making your outside appear "with it" while your inside is a mess, repent of this
- Confess any pride and hypocrisy to your accountability partner
- Sit in a quiet place and ask the Lord to examine every part of you and to point out anything that is displeasing to Him

MATTHEW 24

START HERE

Biblical prophecy provides some of the greatest encouragement and hope available to us today. Just as the Old Testament is saturated with prophecies concerning Christ's first coming, so both Testaments are filled with references to the second coming of Christ.

One scholar has estimated that there are 1,845 references to Christ's second coming in the Old Testament, with seventeen books giving it prominence. Meanwhile, in the two hundred and sixty chapters of the New Testament, there are three hundred and eighteen references to the Second Coming of Christ--an amazing one out of every thirty verses.

Twenty-three of the twenty-seven New Testament books refer to this great event. For every prophecy in the Bible concerning Christ's first advent, there are eight which look forward to His second![21]

CONSIDER

The end times. When we think about Jesus' return, two things should be at the forefront of our minds. First, anyone who doesn't know Christ on that last day will be banished to Hell for eternity. Second, we should not want to be caught doing anything sinful and wrong when the Lord returns.

Keeping Christ's second coming in mind will help us continually remember to share the Gospel and to keep watch over our thoughts, words, choices, attitudes, and actions, so we can be found pleasing the Lord when He returns.

As you read, consider how ready you, and those around you, are for the Lord's return.

READ: MATTHEW 24

INVEST

In verse 12, Jesus states that during the last days there will be famines, wars, natural disasters, and "sin will be rampant everywhere." How is all of that true for today?

Look at again at verse 30. It says there will be "deep mourning among all the peoples of the earth" because when Christ returns it will be too late for repentance. What are you doing to expand the Kingdom before that day comes?

What are verses 42-51 saying?

Why do you think Jesus says to "keep watch" and "be ready at all times" in this section?

How are you doing at being a "faithful, sensible servant" while you await Christ's return?

What more could you do be doing? What might you need to stop doing?

PRAY
- Thank God for those who shared the Gospel with you
- Confess, if necessary, not thinking much about what will happen to those around you when Christ returns
- Ask the Lord to use you to expand His Kingdom while you await the Second Coming
- Ask the Lord to deepen your desire to please Him every moment of every day

TRAINING
- Remember to keep praying over your list of five friends, relatives, co-workers, classmates, and/or neighbors who you know are not saved
- Find a ministry to invest in
- Check out www.operationworld.org. This website provides a different country to pray for each day. It also includes interesting facts and statistics about that country as well as specific prayer requests

MATTHEW 25

START HERE

Jesus plainly declares everyone who ever lived will one day stand before Him. At that time, all of humanity will be separated into two groups. On the right will be those who followed Jesus, and on the left will be those who did not.

What will it be like to stand with those on the right and hear the God of the universe invite you to spend eternity with Him in paradise? It will be unspeakably amazing! But what if you see a friend, a relative, a co-worker, or a neighbor standing over on the left? What will it be like to see their horrified faces when Jesus tells them where they are going? What will it be like to hear their agonizing cries, their begging for one final chance?

What will it be like if those people see you over on the right and cry out, "Why didn't you tell me?!? You obviously knew the right way, why didn't you let me know?!?" What will that be like? I think it will be unspeakably gut-wrenching.

I guarantee when that day comes, you won't be thinking, "I should have played more video games." "I didn't get to watch enough TV." "I should have spent more time on the internet." "Why didn't I earn more money?" "I didn't get to golf enough."

No, you won't be thinking like that at all. Instead, you will be grieving all the missed opportunities and all the lost chances. You'll be devastated by the fact that you left the truth of Hell in your blind spot and kept on driving down the road of life without even giving eternity a second thought.

We can no longer afford to keep the truth of Hell in our blind spot. Instead, we must live each day as though Christ will come back the next. How our lives would change if we believed the Lord was returning in a mere twenty-four hours!

CONSIDER

Every day, over 153,000 people die around the world. Breaking that down, close to 6,400 die every hour. That equals nearly one hundred and seven a minute (or almost two people every second), with two-thirds going into a Christ-less eternity.

If you checked out the obituaries in your local paper, you would find the names of several people who were alive last week but now are not. One day, one of those names could be a friend, a relative, an associate, a classmate, or a neighbor. One day, you may read their name in that obituary. What will you do when you realize it's too late to bring them to Christ?

As you read, consider if you are using your time and talents to reach the lost before it is too late.

READ: MATTHEW 25

INVEST
Verses 1-13 discuss being prepared for Christ's return. Are you confident that you are ready for Jesus's return?

Are you confident that, up until this point, you have done all that you can to reach the lost for Jesus?

In verses 14-30, the Lord talks about "bags of silver." (In the Greek, the word used is "talent" which is where we get our English word for "talent" or "special ability"). With that in mind, are you using the talents God has given you to expand the Kingdom as the first two servants did?

Is there any part of you that is like the third servant?

If so, what must you do about this?

Verses 31-46 show that it is not enough to say, "I am ready" (verses 1-13) or to have talents available for use (verses 14-30). It's about doing all we can to serve others and show them Christ. How are you doing with this?

As was stated under START HERE, it will be unspeakably amazing to stand with those on Jesus' right and hear the God of the universe invite you to spend eternity with Him in paradise! But what if you see a friend, a relative, a co-worker, or a neighbor standing over on the left? What will it be like to see their horrified faces when Jesus tells them where they are going? What will it be like to hear their agonizing cries, their begging for one final chance? What will it be like if those people see you over on the right and cry out, "Why didn't you tell me?!? You obviously knew the right way, why didn't you let me know?!?" What will that be like?

What can you be doing to avoid grieving missed opportunities and lost chances on that final day?

PRAY
- Thank God for providing a way to salvation through Jesus Christ
- Confess, if necessary, not dedicating yourself to doing all you can for others before it is too late
- Ask the Lord to mold you into someone who is ready for the Last Day
- Ask the Lord to use your gifts, talents, and abilities to reach others for Christ

TRAINING
- The Bible says, in 1 Peter 3:15, that we should be prepared to share the Good News at all times, so take some time to consider what you would say to an unsaved friend, relative, associate, or neighbor
- Consider preparing a 3-minute testimony where you can briefly share with someone what you were like before you met Christ, how you met Christ, and what you are like now after having lived for some time with Christ as Lord of your life
- Keeping praying for the five people on your card

MATTHEW 26:1-46

START HERE
Dear Sir:

I am a bricklayer by trade. On the date of the accident, I was working alone on the roof of a new six-story building. When I completed my work, I discovered that I had about five hundred pounds of bricks left over. Rather than carrying the bricks down by hand, I decided to lower them in a barrel by using a pulley which was attached to the side of the building at the sixth-floor level. Securing the rope at ground level, I went up to the roof, swung the barrel out, and loaded the bricks into it. Then I went back down to the ground and untied the rope, holding it tightly to ensure a slow descent. You will note in block number twenty-two of the claim form that my weight is one hundred and fifty pounds.

Due to my surprise at being jerked off the ground so suddenly, I lost my presence of mind and forgot to let go of the rope. Needless to say, I proceeded up the side of the building at a very rapid rate of speed. In the vicinity of the third floor, I met the barrel coming down. This explains my fractured skull and collarbone. Slowed only slightly, I continued my rapid ascent not stopping until the fingers of my right hand were two knuckles deep into the pulley.

By this time, I had regained my presence of mind and was able to hold tightly to the rope in spite of my pain. At approximately the same time; however, the barrel of bricks hit the ground, and the bottom fell out of the barrel. Devoid of the weight of the bricks, the barrel then weighed approximately fifty pounds. I refer you again to the information in block number twenty-two regarding my weight. As you might imagine, I began a rapid descent down the side of the building. In the vicinity of the third floor, I met the barrel coming up. This accounts for the two fractured ankles and the lacerations of my legs and lower body. This second encounter with the barrel slowed me enough to lessen my injuries when I fell onto the pile of bricks and, fortunately, only three vertebrae were cracked.

I am sorry to report, however, as I lay there on the bricks in pain, I again lost my presence of mind and, again, let go of the rope…[22]

Bad days. We've all had them. So, the question isn't, "Have you ever had a bad day?" No, the real question is, "How do you react to your bad days?"

CONSIDER

As the end draws near for Jesus' earthly ministry, fear, confusion, anger, and doubt seem to reign. The religious leaders are plotting Jesus' death, the disciples are acting immature and selfish, Judas becomes a betrayer, and Christ shudders at the thought of being filled with our sin and separated from the Father.

Nevertheless, in spite of it all, Jesus resolutely stays the course, seeking to honor the Father above all else. As you read, consider how resolute you are to honor God during both ordinary and challenging circumstances.

READ: MATTHEW 26:1-46

INVEST

In verses 1-5, what were the religious leaders doing?

In verses 14-16, what was Judas doing?

In verses 31-34, what does Jesus say Peter will do?

What does Jesus cry out in verse 38?

In spite of His agony, what does Christ add in verses 39 and 42?

How do you react when life is hard, and things get difficult?

As one thing after another swirled both in and around Him, Jesus was sure to pray. What can you learn from this?

PRAY

- Thank God that He is always there to hear you when you cry out to Him in prayer

- Confess, if necessary, turning from God in anger when things get difficult instead of running to Him for comfort
- Ask the Lord to fill you with faith, trust, and hope
- Hand over to God any issue that you are struggling with right now

TRAINING

Prayer is a vital part of life. Consider some of these suggestions to help develop your prayer life:

- If you have not done so, make a list of three to five people you know are not saved. Each morning, pray for those people
- Have a prayer basket on your kitchen table to reference during meals. In the prayer basket in my home, we have a *PrayerPoint* booklet that is available for free through Samaritan's Purse. In it, you will find a different country, state, or organization to pray for every week
- If you have children, pray with them before school, before bed, at meals, and any other time you can think of
- Stay up to date on current events and keep them all in prayer—consider also praying for specific politicians and others in key positions in our country and culture. (I often pray for a select group of actors, musicians, movie directors, etc., trusting God will change their hearts…and thus the fruits of their labor)

MATTHEW 26:47 – 27:10

START HERE

Joseph Mazzella writes, "When I was a young father and Autumn would spread her colorful carpet across the hills and mountains of my home, I would often load my kids into the car and embark on a Fall foliage tour. We would take the back roads and look at the leaves shining in the sunlight. There would be glittering golds, blazing reds, and outrageous oranges, sometimes all on the same tree. We would drive and stop and look and be in awe of the beauty of this world and the glory of God's creation.

I remember one time driving a long way down a back road I was unfamiliar with. At one point I came to a crossroads. Down one lane the road was still paved and looked in good condition. The other road, however, was gravel and didn't look quite so good. Ignoring my better instincts, I decided to take a chance and go down the gravel road. It didn't take long to realize that I had made a big mistake. The road was full of potholes and rocks that dragged under my car. I almost got stuck in the mud once and the road seemed to worsen as I went along. Finally, I stopped the car and looked around. There was no going forward and no place to turn so I decided to put the car in reverse and drive a mile and a half backward until I reached the safety of the crossroads again.

Sadly, that wasn't the only time in my life when I reached a crossroads and took the wrong way. I have done so more times than I can count. Thankfully, each time, with God's guidance, I realized my mistake and put my life in reverse until I was on the right road again.

Herbert O'Driscoll once wrote: 'Crossroads call for choice, and the choices we make will change the pattern of our lives.' There is no shame, though, in changing your choice if you see you are on the wrong road. There is no guilt in reversing your life to make things right. God loves us, guides us, and forgives our mistakes. Choose wisely then. Let God guide your days. Make your choices with love. And correct your mistakes when you need too. Then all of your changes will lead you to joy, and the pattern of your life will become as beautiful as a forest in the Fall."[23]

CONSIDER

As Jesus stays steadfast in His desire to follow God's path, we meet two men at a crossroads. Peter and Judas. Both turn their backs on the Lord. One, however, would repent and change. The other would not.

As you read, consider how you handle failure. Do you repent and seek change, or do you give in and give up?

READ: MATTHEW 26:47-27:10

INVEST
How does Judas betray Jesus in verses 26:48-49?

How does Jesus address him in verse 26:50?

How does Judas handle his sin and failure in verses 27:1-5?

Judas was sorry for his sin of betrayal (verse 27:4), but that sorrow did not lead to repentance and change. When you sin and fail, how do you usually respond?

What does Peter do in verses 26:69-75?

Check out 2 Peter 1:1, how does Peter refer to himself?

How does this show Peter's repentance and change?

For all those who accept Christ as Lord and Savior, there should be a change from selfish to selfless, prideful to humble, willful to slave, and much more. What are you doing to show the change Jesus should make in you?

PRAY
- Thank Jesus for the change He can make in and through you
- Confess, if necessary, being sorry for your sin, but not allowing that "sorry" to lead to repentance and change

- Ask the Lord to transform you from the inside out
- Seek forgiveness wherever necessary

TRAINING
Not sure what it looks like to genuinely repent, look at the five steps below:
- Recognition—Don't excuse, blame, deflect, or rationalize your behavior. Instead, humbly admit you have failed
- Remorse—Let the recognition of sin and failure lead you to true sorrow for your actions. 2 Corinthians 7:10 states, *Godly sorrow brings repentance that leads to salvation and leaves no regret, but worldly sorrow brings death*
- Renunciation—This is where being sorry transforms into being repentant. You know longer want to do, say, or think anything that leads to sin and grieves God's heart. Your desire is for righteous living
- Restitution—Did you hurt someone? Apologize. Did you cost someone something? Pay up. Make right what you did wrong. Seek to heal your relationship with God and with others

MATTHEW 27:11-56

START HERE
President Calvin Coolidge invited some people from his hometown to dinner at the White House. Since they did not know how to behave at such an occasion, they thought the best policy would be just to do what the President did.

The time came for serving coffee. The President poured his coffee into a saucer. As soon as the home folk saw it, they did the same. The next step for the President was to pour some milk and add a little sugar to the coffee in the saucer. The home folks did the same.

They thought for sure that the next step would be for the President to take the saucer with the coffee and begin sipping it. But the President didn't do so. He leaned over, placed the saucer on the floor, and called the cat.

Imitating others is sometimes good and sometimes not. It all depends on the source!

CONSIDER
The culmination of Jesus' earthly ministry is unfolding. All of His life has led to these moments—where He would take the sins of the world upon Himself and die in our place. As the final curtain prepares to drop, several actors take the stage. Each one with a part to play.

As you read, consider how alike or unlike you might be to each of them.

READ: MATTHEW 27:11-56

INVEST
Barabbas was a murderer, rightfully condemned to die for his actions, yet an innocent Jesus would be chosen to die in his place. How does this fact make you very much like Barabbas?

Outside of the Gospels, there is no other mention of Barabbas in the Bible. Moreover, church history makes no mention of him. Perhaps this means being saved by Jesus' death made no impact on his life. How can you make sure the same is not true for you?

Simon the Cyrene became the first person to pick up a cross and follow Christ, as he was selected to take up Jesus' cross and follow Him to Calvary. To honor what Jesus did on your behalf, you, too, should be denying self, picking up the cross, and following. How are you doing with that?

The leading priests and many others mocked and ridiculed Jesus, refusing to follow or believe. Are there times when you refuse to follow Christ and/or the commands of Scripture?

If so, what must you do about this?

The Roman centurion recognized Jesus as the Son of God. If you recognize this, how are you living out that recognition with your actions, words, thoughts, attitudes, and choices?

PRAY
- Thank Jesus for dying on the cross in your place for your sins
- Confess, if necessary, not honoring His sacrifice through right living
- Ask the Lord to use you to spread the Good News of His death and resurrection
- Ask the Lord to glorify Himself in and through you

TRAINING
- Review the language you use, the attitudes you exude, the actions you show, and the behaviors you consistently repeat. Do they all reflect Christ? What may need to change?
- Review the media you ingest. What movies and TV shows do you watch? What music do you listen to? What websites do you frequent? Are these all things that Christ Himself would spend time with?

- Review how you react when wronged, when your children blow it, when your spouse irritates you, when your favorite sports' team is losing, etc. Does your attitude need adjustment in any of these areas?
- Review how often you pray and study Scripture. Consider how you treat Sunday mornings. Do you show excitement to get to church and worship the Lord?
- Review how well you serve your family. How often do they see you sacrificing for them and putting their needs above your own?

MATTHEW 27:57-28:20

START HERE
Consider lines from David Crowder's song, "My Victory."

You came for criminals and every pharisee
You came for hypocrites, even one like me

You carried sin and shame, the guilt of every man
The weight of all I've done, nailed into Your hands

Oh, Your love bled for me
Oh, Your blood in crimson streams
Oh, Your death is hell's defeat
A cross meant to kill is my victory

Oh, Your amazing grace, I've seen and tasted it
It's running through my veins. I can't escape its grip
In You my soul is safe, You cover everything

Oh, Your love bled for me
Oh, Your blood in crimson streams
Oh, Your death is hell's defeat
A cross meant to kill is my victory[24]

CONSIDER
The worst of times becomes the best of times as we shift from Matthew 27 into Matthew 28. Despair becomes rejoicing; loss transforms to victory; death loses its sting, and life bursts forth!

As you read, consider how the cross, once an instrument of fear and torture, is now a symbol of healing, hope, and transformation.

READ: MATTHEW 27:57-28:20

INVEST
Joseph, a religious leader, comes out in public support of Jesus by offering up his own tomb for the Lord's burial. This was a great personal sacrifice, as it

most assuredly ended his "career" as a member of the Sanhedrin. How have you sacrificed for the One who gave up so much for you?

Verse 28:2 gives us a great image. The angel rolls aside the stone and sits right on it! It's a fantastic picture of Christ's victory. Where do you need the Lord's power to bring victory into your life?

What do verses 18-20 state?

How are you going about fulfilling the Great Commission?

What more can you be doing to let others know about the risen Savior?

PRAY
- Thank Jesus for His victory over sin, death, and the grave
- Confess, if necessary, not working to spread the news of Christ's sacrificial death and glorious resurrection
- Ask the Lord to open the hearts of those around you to the truth of the Gospel
- Ask the Lord for the boldness to share the message of salvation with them

TRAINING
- Pick one of the five people on your prayer list and invite him or her out for a meal or coffee
- Pray beforehand that the Lord will give you wisdom and boldness. Consider calling on other prayer warriors to pray as well
- While together with this individual, look for opportunities to share the Gospel

MARK 1

START HERE

While Matthew's Gospel is filled with extended times of teaching, Mark's gospel portrays Jesus as constantly on the move. Thirty-nine times Mark used the word *immediately*, giving a sense that Jesus's time on earth was short and that there was much to accomplish in His few years of ministry.

As we saw in Matthew, Jesus was often portrayed as King. Mark, however, reveals Him as God's Servant. Jesus's work was always for a larger purpose, a point clearly summarized in Mark 10:45, *"For even the Son of Man did not come to be served, but to serve, and to give His life a ransom for many."* Mark filled his gospel with the miracles of Jesus, illustrating again and again both the power and the compassion of the Son of God.[25]

"But Jesus's life as the agent of change wasn't without an ultimate purpose. Amid His hands-on ministry, Jesus constantly pointed to the definitive way in which He would serve humanity: His death on the cross and His resurrection from the dead. It is only through faith in these works of Jesus Christ that human beings find eternal redemption for their whole selves. Moreover, Jesus becomes our model for how to live our lives—serving others as He did."[26]

CONSIDER

Authority. Jesus has it, and it is on full display numerous times as we begin our look at the book of Mark. (Such a great name for a book, don't you think?)

The word *authority* is used of Christ, and seen through Him, as He commands illnesses to vanish, drives demons from the possessed, teaches with power, and dramatically changes lives. Everything in all creation, it seems, submits to Christ's authority…except for people!

As you read, consider how well you humbly submit to God's authority (and the authorities He has placed over you).

READ: MARK 1

INVEST

How does John the Baptist describe Jesus in verse 7?

What do the people say about Jesus in verses 22 and 27?

How does Jesus display His authority throughout chapter 1?

What does Jesus say to the leper in verse 41?

What great news to know that no matter how "unclean" or sinful you are, Jesus desires to reach out and touch you to bring healing and forgiveness into your life! With that in mind, where do you need the Lord's power to go work in you right now?

It is interesting that the leper is commanded *not* to tell anyone about what Jesus did, yet he cannot contain himself. Meanwhile, we have been commanded to tell everyone (see Matthew 28:18-20) and are often silent! With whom can you share the message of what Christ has done in you and your life?

When it comes to humbly obeying Christ, where are you doing well? What areas need some work?

PRAY
- Thank Jesus for His authority over everything
- Confess, if necessary, not humbly submitting to that authority
- Ask the Lord to mold you into a humble servant
- Ask the Lord to work mightily in and through your life

TRAINING
Review the following areas of your life to see how well you are submitting in each:
- Your mind: Do you struggle with lustful thoughts? Bad attitudes? Thinking poorly of others? Pride and ego? Lies? Worry? Do you watch or listen to things that are filled with sexuality, foul language, unbiblical themes, blasphemy, etc.?
- Your body: Are you keeping your body physically fit and in shape?

Are you exercising and eating right? Do you avoid sexual immorality? Do you drink alcohol excessively, smoke, use drugs, or abuse prescription medications?

- Your time: Are you using your time wisely? Do you spend time in the Word, in prayer, in Bible study, in worship, and in service? Are you wasting too much time with hobbies, TV, the internet, the apps on your phone, social media, sports, etc.?

- Your talents: Are you using the gifts, talents, and abilities God has given you for His glory or for your own? Are you taking the passions and desires He has filled your heart with and using them for ministry or for self-advancement?

MARK 2

START HERE

In my devotional, *The Letters of Paul,* I share the following story: It was Christmas Eve, 1910. General William Booth, the founder of the Salvation Army, was near the end of his life. Given his health, it was impossible for him to attend the Army's annual convention.

Someone suggested that he send a telegram to be read at the opening of the convention to the many Salvation Army soldiers in attendance as an encouragement for their dedicated hours of labor serving others throughout the holidays and the cold winter months. Booth agreed.

Funds were limited and telegrams charged by the word, so to ensure as much money as possible would still go to help the needy, General Booth decided to send a one-word message. He searched his mind and reviewed his years of ministry, seeking the one word that would summarize his life and the mission of the Army.

When the thousands of delegates met, the moderator announced that Booth could not be present due to his failing health. Gloom and pessimism swept across the convention floor until the moderator announced that Booth had sent a telegram to be read at the start of the first session. He opened the message and read: "Others!"[27]

CONSIDER

I am sure you are familiar with this famous short poem by Jessica Nelson North.

I had a little tea party
This afternoon at three.
'Twas very small—
Three guests in all—
Just I, myself and me.

Myself ate all the sandwiches,
While I drank up the tea;
'Twas also I who ate the pie
And passed the cake to me.[28]

Many live their lives trying to please their three favorite people—me, myself, and I. However, to be a Christian is to be outwardly focused. As you read, consider if life is more about you or more about others.

READ: MARK 2

INVEST

In verses 1-12, what do the four friends do for their lame friend?

In verse 5, what does Jesus notice about the friends of the paralyzed man?

Who are you bringing to Jesus, through prayer and service, because *your* faith believes if you do these things, the Lord will go to work in their lives?

In verse 15, after Matthew encounters Christ, what does he do for his friends and colleagues?

Matthew wanted his lost friends and associates to meet Christ. How much do you wish to see your unsaved friends, relatives, co-workers, classmates, and neighbors meet Christ?

What more could you be doing for those around you to help them see Christ?

Would you say that you are outwardly focused?

How might you use your time more efficiently to be more other-centered?

PRAY
- Thank the Lord for His desire to reach *all* your friends, relatives, co-workers, classmates, and neighbors
- Confess, if necessary, being more inwardly focused than outwardly

focused
- Ask the Lord to give you a heart that longs to see those around you come to Christ
- Ask the Lord to focus you more on others and less on yourself

TRAINING

Take a moment to assess if you are more outwardly focused or inwardly focused.

- Your prayer time: How much of your prayer time is taken up with issues and concerns involving you or your family compared to how much is taken up praying for the lost, for issues your neighbors, co-workers, and/or classmates are having?
- Your thought life: Do your thoughts revolve mostly around you and your issues, or do you spend time thinking how you might help others, where you can serve, what you can do to connect with your neighbors, etc.?
- Your eyes: Are you always looking around for someone who might seem lonely, sad, struggling, hurting, etc.? Are you always mindful of what is going on around you?
- Your money: Does your income go to your pursuits and hobbies, or are you using the money God has blessed you with to further the Kingdom and bless others?

MARK 3

START HERE
Archaeologists digging in the remains of a school for imperial pages in Rome found a picture dating from the third century. It showed a boy standing, his hand raised, worshiping a figure on a cross—a figure that looked like a man but had the head of a donkey. Scrawled in the writing of a young person were the words, "Alexamenos worships his God." Nearby, in a second inscription, one can see the words: "Alexamenos is faithful."

Apparently, Alexamenos was a young Christian being mocked by his schoolmates for his beliefs. However, the lad did not shrink back; he was faithful.[29] May that be said of us as well.

CONSIDER
In Mark 3, confusion, doubt, anger, and hatred interweave with hope, healing, and new life. Though this chapter was written nearly two thousand years ago, not much has changed! Throughout history, wherever the Gospel goes, Satan and the world actively attack. Because of this, when God's truth is shared, some run to the transforming power of Christ, while others flee or fight it.

As you read, consider if you are willing to deal with anger, doubt, hate, and confusion to see lives changed for eternity.

READ: MARK 3

INVEST
The supporters of Herod were worldly individuals who dismissed much of the Old Testament in order to live for pleasure. Meanwhile, the Pharisees were obsessively careful to obey every letter of God's Law. This put these two groups at absolute odds. However, their mutual hatred of Jesus was so great that they did what in verse 6?

What did Jesus' family say about Him in verse 21?

What do the religious leaders say about Jesus in verse 22?

Through all of this, Jesus continues to heal, teach, and train others to carry on His work. How do you handle it when there is pushback (or worse) for being a Christian?

How might you handle things better than you are currently?

What are you doing for the Kingdom of God right now?

What more could you be doing?

PRAY
- Thank God for those who endure much persecution yet continue steadfastly proclaiming Christ
- Confess, if necessary, backing down too often from sharing God's truth
- Ask the Lord to encourage you to share His truth regardless of what others say or think
- Ask the Lord to show you where He wants to use you to make a difference for His Kingdom

TRAINING
Every day an estimated three hundred people are killed because of their faith in Christ. Here are some ways you can pray for the persecuted church (numbering around two hundred million fellow believers).
- Pray persecuted believers would know the hope God gives
- Pray the Holy Spirit would strengthen them
- Pray persecuted believers would know how much God loves them
- Pray persecuted believers would fearlessly tell others about Jesus
- Pray persecuted believers would have access to a Bible
- Pray for believers who have been rejected by family and friends, that God would surround them with a new Christian "family" that loves them and supports them
- Pray that God would provide persecuted believers with jobs and safe places to live[30]

MARK 4

START HERE

How about we start with some lousy farm jokes.

- Why did the scarecrow win the Nobel Prize? Because he was out standing in his field!
- What do you get when you cross a robot and a tractor? A trans-farmer.
- What day do potatoes hate the most? Fry-day!
- Did you hear about the magic tractor? It turned into a field!
- What do farmers use to make crop circles? A Pro-tractor
- Where do farmers send their kids to grow? Kinder-garden.
- Who tells chicken jokes? Comedi-hens!
- What is a farmer's favorite Bruce Springsteen song? Born in the USDA.
- Why did the police arrest the turkey? They suspected it of fowl play.
- What did the farmer get when he crossed an owl with a goat? A 'Hootinanny'[31]

Why did I ruin your day with the corniest (no pun intended) jokes ever? Well, today, we are talking about a farmer scattering seed. Seventy-five percent of those seeds ended up worse than these jokes. Let's hope we are all like the other twenty-five percent.

CONSIDER

It is sadly not uncommon for someone to pray at an altar one time and then conclude, "I am good to go." However, you will search the Bible in vain for a place where Jesus says, "Hey, if you want to be My disciple, meet Me up front at the end of My sermon, pray a prayer with Me, and then I'll see you in Heaven!"

There are, however, numerous Scripture references where we are challenged to daily sacrifice, surrender, learn, and mature. As you read, consider what it really means to be "saved."

READ: MARK 4

INVEST
In verses 1-20, what do each of the four seeds represent?

Why are study and growth important for a Christian according to verses 17, 24, and 25?

Look again at verses 18 and 19. Are there times when you are guilty of being like this seed?

What tends to distract and detour you from producing fruit?

What will it take for you to be the seed that produces thirty, sixty, or even one hundred times as much as was planted in you?

PRAY
- Thank God for those who planted the seeds of faith in you
- Confess, if necessary, being one (or more) of the first three seeds
- Ask the Lord to grow, deepen, and mature you as a Christian
- Ask the Lord to use you to produce a mighty harvest

TRAINING
Consider these five ways to develop your walk with the Lord:
- Attend church on a weekly basis. Make church a priority on Sundays and don't allow kids' sports, hobbies, and more to keep you from worship each week
- Join a small group and surround yourself with believers who will hold you accountable, help you grow, and keep you in prayer
- Read your Bible daily. Feed on God's Word regularly to grow in grace and truth
- As 1 Thessalonians 5:17 declares, *pray without ceasing*. Be in a constant state of prayer throughout the day
- Find ways to serve the Lord, using the talents and gifts He has blessed you with. We grow closer God as we live out our created purpose
- Share your faith. Look for opportunities to give the Good News

MARK 5

START HERE

In Mark 5, Jesus encounters a man filled with evil! In Bible times, a Roman legion was composed of five thousand men. So, if the demons are calling themselves "Legion," then how much evil is infesting this man? There is evil beyond scope, so much evil in fact that it cannot be contained. We read that the townsfolk tried to shackle him in chains, but the intense power of evil inside Legion broke free every time. So much evil pervaded this man that the Bible even says no one was strong enough to control him. Did you catch that? No one!

Isn't that the case with the evil inside of us? We have all tried with our own human measures to control sin. We have all tried in our own feeble strength to constrain our actions, our words, and our thoughts. We have all tried and tried—and failed and failed—because we do not have the power to deal effectively with the sin and evil in our lives. They are far too strong for us, and so we continue to inflict more and more damage on ourselves and others. Isn't that what happened with Legion as he terrorized the town folk and hit himself with stones?

The situation seemed hopeless for Legion. That is until Jesus showed up. Seeing Jesus and the disciples hit the shore, Legion presumably runs to terrorize them as he did so many others. Yet, when he reaches Jesus, all Legion can do is fall to his knees and beg not to be tortured. Sin and evil are no match for Jesus! He has the power to break the hold of evil, the power to cancel sin, and the power to set us free from the things that bind us.

CONSIDER

Got problems? Mark 5 has answers.

Without a doubt, problems abound both within and without. Our hearts seem drawn to sin. Meanwhile, we are surrounded by others who are just as fallen as we are, and their choices often negatively affect our lives. So, no matter how you slice it, problems *will* come our way. The question is, how will we handle them?

As you read, consider what you do when problems come your way. Do you give them over to Jesus or try to handle them in your own strength?

READ: MARK 5

INVEST

As we discussed in START HERE, Legion is busy hurting himself and others (verses 4-5), and *no one* has the power to do anything about it, then Jesus shows up with more than enough power to defeat Legion and his legion of problems. With that in mind, do you turn to Jesus with your issues, or do you end up hurting yourself and others as you strive in vain to handle them yourself?

If you are guilty of trying to handle life's problems by yourself, what must you do?

The woman bleeding for twelve years had tried everything in her power and resources to fix the problem with nothing to show for it except an empty bank account and worse symptoms. But what happened when she grabbed hold of Jesus?

In the middle of a seemingly hopeless situation, Jairus heard Jesus say, "Don't be afraid. Just have faith." How did he respond?

What do you think will consistently happen if you give your problems to Jesus and trust Him with the results?

PRAY

- Thank Jesus for His ability to bring hope to any "hopeless" situation
- Confess, if necessary, trying to handle problems by yourself
- Give to the Lord any problems or issues you are dealing with right now
- Ask the Lord to work in the lives of others you know who are struggling with difficult situations

TRAINING

Do you truly believe Jesus has the power to forgive your sins, purge your past, and bring lasting solutions to your struggles? Do you really, truly believe that? If Jesus can do it for Legion and for legions of others, He can do it for you. The only thing stopping you from experiencing all that Christ has to offer *is you.*

Others may try to dissuade you from giving yourself over to Christ, and Satan may try to lead you down empty paths, but ultimately the choice is yours. Either you choose to surrender to the power of Christ, or you choose not to. No one else makes that choice for you. You and you alone own that choice.

What will you choose?

MARK 6

START HERE

In the Fall of 2014, I coached a community football team that went 10-0. It was the first team from that league to ever go undefeated. Quite an accomplishment. And those players, all kids in their early to mid-teens, were definitely pleased with themselves. (Perhaps, *over-pleased* would be a better word.)

The next year, this team had the opportunity to join a different league that promised a stronger class of competition. My players were all firmly convinced they would dominate that league as well.

Knowing that the level of play would be more intense, practice leading up to the start of that season stayed energized and focused. After a win in the lone pre-season week, however, practices quickly dropped in intensity and focus. The boys were sure it was going to be another cake walk. Eight weeks later, we were 3-5.

They say practice makes perfect. That is certainly true in sports, in life, and also in our faith.

CONSIDER

In Mark 5, we saw a sharp contrast between what we can do versus what God can do. As we head into chapter 6, that contrast continues. Even though it should be obvious that the Lord can handle things much better than we can, still we try to deal with much of life's struggles in our own strength and means.

Oh sure, some things seem well within our control, so we fall into the trap of "we got this!" Only, we don't "got this." Sooner or later, a trial comes barreling into our lives, threatening to knock us square on our bum. Instead of rising in faith and trust, we fall into despair, because we've only practiced handling things on our own.

I can tell you, as someone who has coached sports for over twenty-five seasons, "You play like you practice." It's no different in life. So, as you read, consider how well you are practicing your faith. Are you practiced at giving all your cares, trials, and struggles to the Lord, or are you practiced at stubbornly trying to handle everything yourself?

READ: MARK 6

INVEST

What did Jesus give the disciples in verse 7?

According to verse 13, what could the disciples accomplish with Jesus' authority?

Even though it was Jesus' power and authority at work through the disciples, what do the twelve say in verse 30?

Jesus, in back to back events, works to show the disciples that everything accomplished was not because of what "they had done." To start emphasizing this, what does He tell them to do for the large crowd in verse 37?

How do they respond in that same verse?

In verse 45, the Bible says that Jesus made (literally "compelled" or "insisted") the disciples get in their boats and head to the other side of the lake. Why do you think He was so insistent?

Do you tend to try to handle life's issues your way in your strength?

What lessons can you take from Mark 6?

What do you need to put into Jesus' hands right now?

PRAY
- Thank God that He is more than able to handle anything that comes thundering into your life
- Confess, if necessary, stubbornly believing you can handle things your

way in your strength
- Ask the Lord to humble you
- Give the Lord any issue or struggle you are dealing with right now

TRAINING
- Ask yourself if you are daily tapping into the Lord's power. If you have trusted Christ as your Lord and Savior, then that power surely resides within you. The question isn't, "Do I have this power?" The question is, "Am I using this power?"
- It is not a power to get rich, to have a problem-free existence, or to gain fame and stardom. It is beyond that. It is a power which overcomes your fears, cancels sin, restores relationships, frees from addiction, and does infinitely more than you can ever ask or imagine
- Time to practice using that power. Don't you think?

MARK 7

START HERE

In December of 1944, General Anthony C. McAuliffe commanded the 101st Airborne during the Battle of Bastogne. Germany launched one last offensive (known as the Battle of the Bulge) and surrounded the city of Bastogne. The German Commander, General Heinrich von Luettwitz called for McAuliffe to surrender. Outraged, McAuliffe sent off his now famous one-word reply. "NUTS!"

Even with translators, the Germans had difficulty understanding this 1940s version of "Up yours!" Meanwhile, McAuliffe and his forces were able to hold off the German siege until the 4th Armored Division arrived to provide reinforcements.

We love these stories, don't we? A battle-hardened general scoffing at the notion of surrendering to an advancing enemy force. Our hearts shout, "Yes! Stand up! Fight! Don't give in. Don't give up. Never surrender!"

Of course, when it comes to standing up for your country, your people, and your principles, it is crucial to stay the course and never give up or give in. I applaud those who do that on a daily basis. Yet, if we let this idea seep into our relationship with Jesus, then we have a serious problem. Because when it comes to truly knowing and experiencing more of Christ, surrender is the key.

CONSIDER

Did I mention that when it comes to truly knowing and experiencing more of Christ, surrender is the key?

Good. Because we will never truly know and experience Jesus Christ without first surrendering totally, completely, and unreservedly to Him. This reality, however, is the last thing many of us want to do. Sure, we might be willing to surrender some things to Him. I mean, after all, we know that there are things in our lives that need work, and so we gladly give them over to Christ. But Jesus says, "No, I don't just want parts of you. I want all of you. Don't give yourself to Me in pieces. Give Me everything."

The problem is we don't want to give everything. There are things we are keeping a firm grasp on, and no one is going to pry them from our hands. Maybe it's a relationship. You know it doesn't honor God, but you don't want to give it up. Maybe it's a job. You have to cut corners sometimes, but you need the money. Maybe it's a habit. You know it is affecting your relationship with the Lord, but you like it too much to give it up. Maybe it's entertainment choices. You know you shouldn't let Hollywood influence your time and life so much, but can't a guy relax in front of the tube for a couple of hours every night? It could be one of a million things that you know you should give up, but, quite frankly, you just don't want to.

In Mark 7, one of the things that the Pharisees won't surrender is their traditions. As you read, consider what it is you won't surrender.

READ: MARK 7

INVEST
In verses 6-8, how does Jesus respond to the Pharisees complaining about their traditions not being followed?

Are there places in your life where you ignore God's Word and substitute your thoughts, traditions, and choices?

In verses 15-23, how does Jesus show we must surrender anything that can clutter and defile our hearts?

On a scale of one to ten, with one being "terrible" and ten being "Fort Knox," rate how well you guard your heart. Explain your rating:

At first glance, verses 24-30 seem to show Jesus a bit condescending and rude. In actuality, the opposite is occurring as Jesus again works to get people to surrender false notions, ideas, and traditions. It was unthinkable for a Jewish teacher to instruct Gentiles and even more unthinkable for that teacher to talk publicly to a Gentile woman. Yet, Jesus is teaching in a Gentile land, publicly addressing a Gentile woman. As only Jesus can do, He is simultaneously testing the woman's faith and breaking down barriers and misconceptions at the same time. What kind of barriers should Christians be breaking down today?

What things do you need to surrender to be fully committed to Christ and His Kingdom?

PRAY
- Thank Jesus for breaking down walls and barriers
- Confess, if necessary, a refusal to surrender things that are keeping you from God's best
- Ask the Lord to strengthen your commitment to Him
- Ask the Lord to examine every part of your life and reveal to you anything that needs surrendering

TRAINING
- Think about what you need to surrender to the Lord
- Ask yourself if you are willing to follow the Lord wherever, whenever, and with whatever
- Spend time in prayer, asking the Lord to work in and through your life
- Take inventory of your music collection, movie collection, video game collection, web browser history, etc., and ask yourself what needs to go
- Get an accountability partner to help you stay surrendered

MARK 8

START HERE

Perhaps you have been beaten up pretty bad in this life, or perhaps life hasn't been all that bad. Maybe others have let you down too many times to count, or maybe people, in general, have been good to you. I don't know what your situation is, but I do know this. Jesus can be trusted. In fact, He is the only one who can be entirely trusted. Unlike us fallible humans, He is God and He is perfect.

This means He is perfectly trustworthy and His success rate in dealing with sins, hurts, pasts, and problems is 100%. Your next step then is to place yourself completely in His hands. You must make it a daily prayer to entrust your life wholly to Christ. Time to stop trying to handle everything yourself. It can't be done.

We might fool ourselves into thinking we can handle life by ourselves, but then it happens. That sin we cannot conquer; that job we cannot keep; that bill we cannot pay; that disease we cannot cure; that loved one we cannot help; that death we cannot stop. It happens to us all. When it happens to you, will you be found alone or in the arms of Christ? One is a much better place than the other!

Trust Christ with everything in your life. He has all the power you need and more. Through His immeasurable power, you will find victory over sin, success over past failures, triumph over loss, and hope amid despair. Don't crawl through life in your own strength, when you can soar in Christ's strength.

CONSIDER

The main reason I have trust issues is that oatmeal raisin cookies look way too much like chocolate chip cookies! Has anyone else literally tasted disappointment as I have with this?

Many of us would not admit to having trust issues with Jesus, but what happens when life seems hard and nothing is going right? Or what happens when Jesus says, "Trust me enough to deny yourself, pick up your cross, and follow"? Do you trust unreservedly or pause?

The disciples would probably not admit to having trust issues with Jesus either. However, in Mark 8, a lack of faith is on full display. As you read, consider how deeply you trust Jesus to guide, provide, and bless your life.

READ: MARK 8

INVEST
Jesus just fed a more massive crowd in chapter 6, yet how do the disciples react in verse 4?

In a very short period, Jesus miraculously fed two *huge* groups of people. You'd think by now the disciples would have gained a bit of trust. However, why are they arguing in verse 16?

What does Jesus say about all of this in verses 17-21?

Jesus was more than capable of instantly healing the blind man in verses 22-26. However, He healed him in stages to act out an object lesson for the disciples. They were like the man who went from being blind to "kind of seeing" while not really seeing clearly at all. How might you be like this man, failing to completely see what Christ can do if you fully surrendered to Him?

What does Jesus say in verses 34-36?

How are you doing at this?

What needs some work?

PRAY
- Thank Jesus for how awesome and amazing He truly is
- Confess, if necessary, not fully trusting Him with your life
- Give the Lord your life, your whole life

- Ask the Lord to fill you with faith and trust

TRAINING
- Spend a few moments reviewing times when you tried in vain to handle everything yourself
- Confess to Christ, if necessary, the times you have neglected His work in your life
- Pray over some issues in your life that you have been trying to handle by yourself. Give them over to Christ and allow His power to work
- Pledge yourself to Christ. Put yourself in His hands and work to keep Him at the center of your life

MARK 9

START HERE

Let's face it. If we make it our goal to seek more in Jesus and not more in the world, we just put ourselves in the center of Satan's crosshairs. I don't say this to frighten you. I just want you to know the reality of it. The devil hates Jesus Christ and wants nothing less than everyone spending eternity separated from the Lord's presence. Heaven to be empty and Hell to be full is Satan's goal. When we purpose to center on Christ and lead others to do likewise, we set ourselves in direct opposition to that goal.

Since this is true, you can take it to the bank that the devil will assail you with doubts and questions. He wants you to question God's love for you. He wants you to distrust God's will. He wants you to wonder if Jesus is really who He says He is. He wants you to be skeptical of the Bible's accuracy and authority. He wants you to be uncertain of your convictions. He wants you to be filled with pride and hesitate to trust that Christ can manage your life much better than you can. He wants all that and much more.

Again, I don't tell you this to scare you but to make you aware of how Satan works. The Apostle Paul told the Corinthians to be mindful of these things *so that Satan [would] not outsmart us. For we are very familiar with his evil schemes.*[32] It is important that we too be familiar with the devil's evil schemes. That way, when doubts, uncertainty, pride, or embarrassment well up within us, we will know the source of that flow.

CONSIDER

In chapter 9, lack of faith, excessive doubt, and crippling uncertainty form a devastating triumvirate. The Pharisees, the bulk of the general population, and even the twelve disciples continue to miss who Jesus really is and what He came to do in and through them.

As you read, consider how solid your faith and trust in the Lord is.

READ: MARK 9

INVEST

What does God say in verse 7 to confirm who Jesus is?

What does Jesus say about the disciples (and others) in verse 19?

What does Jesus say to the doubting father in verse 23?

What does the Bible say about the disciples in verse 32?

Like God did for Peter, James, and John, He often does for us. Again and again, through various ways, the Lord confirms He can be trusted. What are some ways the Lord has done this for you?

In spite of these things, do you still have doubts and uncertainties from time to time?

If you answered "yes," what must you do with these things?

The devil is the father of lies and the author of doubt, so what can you do to keep him at bay?

PRAY
- Thank God for the truth of His Word
- Confess, if necessary, struggling with doubts
- Ask the Lord to assure you of His goodness, faithfulness, and love
- Ask the Lord to cast out fear, doubt, and uncertainty

TRAINING
- Mentally prepare yourself for the devil's attacks. Don't fear them. God is greater than anything Satan can throw at you. Just know it is coming
- Work to draw close to God. Set aside a daily time to pray and study Scripture to help you bring you near to His presence
- Find a group of others to gather with you who will help you draw close to Christ

MARK 10

START HERE

START HERE

If only I had a little humility, then I would be perfect.

A truly humble man is hard to find, yet God delights to honor such selfless people. Booker T. Washington, the renowned black educator, was an outstanding example of this truth.

Shortly after he took over the presidency of Tuskegee Institute in Alabama, he was walking in an exclusive section of town when a wealthy white woman stopped him. Not knowing the famous Mr. Washington by sight, she asked if he would like to earn a few dollars by chopping wood for her.

Because he had no pressing business at the moment, Professor Washington smiled, rolled up his sleeves, and proceeded to do the humble chore she had requested. When he finished, he carried the logs into the house and stacked them by the fireplace.[33]

I wonder if I would have reacted the same way Booker did. Probably not. Yet, humility and servanthood were marks of Christ and should be marks of His people as well.

CONSIDER

Central to the Christian life is putting yourself last. Throughout the Gospels (including Mark 10), the disciple consistently failed at this. Of course, it is easy to look at the twelve's failures and shake our heads. However, as you read, consider if you consistently put God and others ahead of yourself or if you are usually number one in your heart.

READ: MARK 10

INVEST

Going back a chapter, what does Jesus say in verse 9:35?

In Mark 10, the rich young man refused to follow Jesus into that kind of lifestyle. Why does verse 22 say that is so?

List a few reasons why some people are unwilling to put God and others ahead of themselves:

How do verses 29-31 and 45 reflect what Jesus was saying in verse 9:35?

When Jesus encounters blind Bartimaeus, He is on His way to Jerusalem preparing to die a torturous death for the sins of the world. So, if anyone had an excuse to say, "I can't help you. I have a lot on my mind right now," it was Jesus. However, what does He say to Bartimaeus in verse 51?

On a scale of one to ten, with one being "totally selfish" and ten being "totally selfless," rate yourself, then explain your rating.

If you rated yourself less than a ten, what more should you be doing?

PRAY
- Thank Jesus for putting you above Himself and dying on the cross in your place
- Confess, if necessary, keeping yourself first
- Ask the Lord to reorder your priorities so that He is first, others are second, and you are last
- Ask the Lord to fill you with a servant's heart and a selfless spirit

TRAINING
- Use the acronym JOY—Jesus, Others, Yourself
- Write it down and place it where you will see it often so that you can be constantly reminded to keep things in their proper order

MARK 11

START HERE

In 1884 a young man died. After the funeral, his grieving parents decided to establish a memorial to him. With that in mind, they met with Charles Eliot, president of Harvard University. Eliot received the unpretentious couple into his office and asked what he could do.

When they expressed their desire to fund a memorial, Eliot impatiently said, "Perhaps you have in mind a scholarship."

"We were thinking of something more substantial than that...perhaps a building," the woman replied.

In a patronizing tone, Eliot brushed aside the idea as being too expensive, and the couple departed. The next year, Eliot learned that this plain pair had gone elsewhere and established a twenty-six million dollar memorial named Leland Stanford Junior University, better known today as Stanford![34]

Unfortunately, stories of unpretentious people are relatively rare. More unfortunate, stories of pretentious people abound!

CONSIDER

Looking good versus being good.

It isn't difficult to pull off looking good in front of others. It is not so easy, however, to consistently live in a way that honors the Lord with our choices, actions, attitudes, thoughts, words, etc.

Stepping into chapter 11, Jesus is going to act out another parable by cursing a fig tree that looked good from a distance, but on closer inspection was fruitless. As you read, consider if you try to look good on the outside more than striving to be good on the inside.

READ: MARK 11

INVEST

On that Palm Sunday, what were the crowds doing in verses 8-10 (even though four days later many of those people would be shouting for Jesus to be crucified)?

From the outside, the Temple looked like a place that honored God, but what was going on inside in verses 15-17?

The leading priests would have looked to all the world like faithful servants of God, but what were they plotting in verse 18?

How does the cursing of the fig tree, in verses 12-14, illustrate what is going on in this chapter?

Today, we can go to church and praise Jesus on Sunday (as the crowd did on Palm Sunday), then during the week reject Jesus by how we live (as the same crowd would do that week). What can you do to guard against this?

Each morning, most of us will shower, put on clean clothes, comb our hair, shave or put on make-up, etc., because we want our outward appearance to be presentable. But what about the inside? What are you doing each day to make sure your inside is right with the Lord?

PRAY
- Thank God for His ability to transform you from the inside out
- Confess, if necessary, a greater focus on your outward appearance than your inward condition
- Ask the Lord to help you be diligent in guarding your heart
- Ask the Lord to transform you from the inside out

TRAINING
- Ask Jesus to make you more like Himself. Ask Him to show you where you fall short and where changes need to be made
- Discipline yourself to set aside daily time for prayer and Bible study
- Change your schedule, if necessary, so you can make it to church each

Sunday and be part of a weekly small group

- Set aside personal objectives and goals. Invest and commit to God's objectives and goals
- If you are not an active part of a Bible-believing church, ask the Lord to guide you to such a church. Ask Him to help you fully invest in that body that you might more fully know His will for your life and more fully reflect His Son Jesus

MARK 12

START HERE

Famous last words:

- What does this button do?
- It's probably just a rash
- Yeah, I'm sure the power is off
- I made the deciding vote on the jury, so what of it?
- The odds of that happening to me have to be a million to one!
- Pull the pin and count to what?
- Which wire was I supposed to cut?
- I wonder where the mother bear is
- Don't worry. I've seen this done on TV lots of times
- No, these are the good kind of mushrooms
- I'll hold it, and you light the fuse
- Get on. It's strong enough for both of us
- This doesn't taste right
- Nice doggie!
- I think it's just the pilot light. Anyone have a match?

Indeed, some last words are better than others!

CONSIDER

A person's last words, last sermon preached, or last class taught is usually a big deal. That individual understands he or she has just one more chance to convey a message. For Jesus, in chapter 12, He knows that His earthly ministry is coming to an end, so He works to clarify who He is and what we should do in response to that knowledge.

As you read, consider your response to all that Jesus is about to say.

READ: MARK 12

INVEST

The evil farmers were given much to use and enjoy. However, they pridefully wanted it all for themselves. Have you been guilty of keeping the time, talents, and treasures (money) God has blessed you with to yourself, or are you using them to build the Kingdom and benefit others?

According to verses 29-31, what are the two most important commandments?

How are you doing at living out these commandments?

Many believe they have little to offer God and so offer nothing at all. In verses 41-44, however, the poor widow gave all she had even though it was a pittance. Are you faithfully giving all that you are (and have) to the Lord?

What can you offer that you have been holding back?

PRAY
- Thank Jesus that He held nothing back and gave all of Himself on the cross for you
- Confess, if necessary, not giving your all for the Lord
- Ask the Lord to help you surrender every part of your life to Him
- Ask the Lord to reveal what areas are still not surrendered

TRAINING
The answer to more fulfillment, deeper satisfaction, and enduring purpose is not found in things, no matter how many of those things you may happen to have. The answer is found in Christ.

If you seem to be continually coming up empty, perhaps it is because you have not been searching for more in Christ. If your life is not infused with purpose, perhaps it is because you have been dipping your bucket into the world's well instead of God's well. If so, it's time to drop your bucket into the vast ocean of God's grace, Christ's love, and the Spirit's infilling.

Your next step is to look to Christ, to seek more of Him, and to understand His will for you right now. Fall on your knees, crawl into the lap of your Heavenly Father, and cry out, "Lord, give me more of Your Son. Fill me with more of Christ. Begin to use me to do more than I ever thought possible."

MARK 13

START HERE
Breaking news! The Second Coming has been cancelled due to lack of interest.

While the above may be a joke, there is definitely some truth to it. Don't stone me yet! Jesus is indeed coming back. Yet, how many are really focused on that fact? Certainly, the Left Behind movies haven't helped our cause (especially the Nicholas Cage one that amazingly climbed all the way to one percent on the www.rottentomatoes.com Tomato Meter. And let's face it. One percent is being generous!)

But really, it is so easy to get wrapped up in our own lives and our own issues. Not to mention that we are surrounded by distractions, with our thoughts and faces buried in our phones, the Internet, TV, and more. Nevertheless, the truth remains. Much of the world is still in need of the Gospel message before Jesus' return.

How much time have you spent sharing that message?

CONSIDER
Be ready while helping others get ready. That is the message of chapter 13. One day, Jesus will be returning to judge the living and the dead. On that day, all we did for eternity will be rejoiced over, while all we did for ourselves will be lamented as wasted time.

As you read, consider which words, deeds, actions, or attitudes from your life will be rejoiced over (and lamented over) on that last day.

READ: MARK 13

INVEST
What does Jesus say in verses 33, 35, and 36?

In those verses, the Lord uses words like "be on guard," "stay alert," and "keep watch." Why do you think He does that?

How well are you keeping watch and staying alert for opportunities to bless others and build the Kingdom?

How well are you guarding against wasted-time, poor choices, and Satan's temptations?

On a scale of one to ten, with one being "not at all" and ten being "bring it," rate how ready you are for Jesus to return? Explain your rating:

If you lived each day like Jesus could come back tomorrow, would that change anything about how you go about your life right now?

If so, how? If not, why not?

PRAY
- Thank God for the opportunities He gives you to make a difference in this world
- Confess, if necessary, not seizing the opportunities that God provides
- Ask the Lord to help you keep watch and stay alert for the opportunities that abound around you
- Ask the Lord to help you be on guard against things that can dampen your faith or distract you from your calling and purpose

TRAINING
In Colossians 4:2, the apostle Paul writes, *devote yourselves to prayer with an alert mind and a thankful heart*. The word used for "devote" in that verse literally means "steadfastly attentive." With that in mind, one way to practice keeping watch and staying alert is to always be on the lookout for opportunities to pray.
- Before the kids go to school, you can pray with them and for them
- At the dinner table, pray as a family
- Your son comes home from school crying because his best friend shunned him. Pray with your child right at that moment
- You see an ambulance with sirens on while driving somewhere, pray

for God to work in that situation
- You're at an event, and someone gets hurt. Pray right there
- You see a terrible story on the news. Start praying
- You get an email that a neighbor is in the hospital. Pray

Always be alert and ready to offer up prayers.

MARK 14:1-42

START HERE

On January 6, 1850, a snowstorm crippled the city of Colchester, England. A teenage boy, fighting the biting wind and squalls, was searching for a church. The fierce weather did not deter him, for the storm in his soul was churning stronger than the storm around him.

That boy would later write. "When I could go no further, I turned down a side street and came to a little Primitive Methodist Chapel…The minister did not come that morning; he was snowed up, I suppose. At last a very thin looking man, a shoemaker or tailor or something of that sort, went up into the pulpit to preach. He read from Isaiah 45:22, *Look unto me, and be ye saved, all the ends of the earth: for I am God, and there is none else.*"

"The preacher bungled the pronunciation. 'My dear friends,' he started, 'this is a very simple text indeed. It says, 'Look.' Now lookin' don't take a deal of pains. It ain't liftin' your foot or your finger; it is just 'look.' Well, a man needn't go to college to learnt to look. You may be the biggest fool, and yet you can look. A man needn't be worth a thousand a year to be able to look. Anyone can look; even a child can look. But then the text says, 'Look unto Me.' Ay! Many on ye are lookin' to yourselves, but it's no use lookin' there. You'll never find any comfort in yourselves. Jesus Christ says, 'Look unto Me.' Look to Christ. The text says, 'Look unto Me.'"

The teen thought the fill-in preacher had said all he had to say, when to his great surprise, the thin man looked straight at him and shouted, "Young man, you look very miserable, and you always will be miserable, miserable in life and miserable in death if you don't obey my text. But if you obey now, this moment, you will be saved. Young man, look to Jesus Christ. Look. You have nothin' to do but to look and live."

The young man records, "I looked until I could almost have looked my eyes away. There and then the cloud was gone, the darkness had rolled away, and that moment I saw the sun, and I could have risen that instant and sung with the most enthusiastic of them, of the precious blood of Christ and the simple faith which looks alone to Him."

That young man was Charles Haddon Spurgeon, one of the greatest preachers of the nineteenth century.

CONSIDER

The mental stress and torture that Jesus was experiencing the night before His impending arrest and death must have been agonizing. Yet, through it all, the Lord continues to teach and bless the disciples while maintaining a steadfast focus on fulfilling God's will.

As you read, consider what you focus on when things get tough? Do you tend to focus on yourself and your issues, or do you look to Christ for His care and provision?

READ: MARK 14:1-42

INVEST

In chapter 14, the only person, besides Jesus, not thinking about himself or herself is the woman with the essence of nard. What does she do?

In Bible times, Romans typically sold the flowers which made nard at today's equivalent of four thousand dollars per pound! In other words, this woman's gift to Jesus was incredibly expensive and deeply sacrificial. How willing are you to sacrifice deeply for the Lord?

Contrasting this woman who gave so extravagantly to the Lord is Judas, who took so very little to betray Jesus. (Thirty pieces of silver would be today's equivalent of two hundred dollars.) It is easy to come down hard on Judas, but it is not uncommon for us to trade in time serving the Lord or growing in Him for time with TV, movies, the internet, video games, hobbies, and other things that are so insignificant compared to time with Christ. Are you guilty of this? If so, how so?

If so, what can you do about it?

What do the bread and the wine at the Last Supper represent?

How wonderful is it to know all that Christ would give up for you?

115

What can you do to honor that sacrifice?

PRAY
- Thank the Lord for His priceless sacrifice
- Confess, if necessary, offering Christ comparatively little in return
- Ask the Lord to imbue you with a desire to give Him your all
- Ask the Lord to help you use your time wisely

TRAINING
- Ask yourself some questions, "Will I live for my own goals, comfort, and pleasure; or will I live for Christ and His glory?" "How might my priorities need to be adjusted?"
- Evaluate how you have been spending your time over the last few weeks. Understand that if Jesus is the reason for everything, you cannot be content with free time spent solely for self
- Continually remind yourself that this world is not your home and that everything in the world that you hold so dear will pass away
- Consider how you are reflecting Christ. Is the reflection pointed straight back at yourself or are you shining outwardly for Christ?
- Consider how much of your life is surrendered to the Lord. Is it one hundred percent? If not, what parts have yet to be surrendered?

MARK 14:43-72

START HERE
Think of all the stories that we have seen in Matthew and Mark where people look to Jesus and find hope. The woman with the wound that hemorrhaged and oozed for twelve long years. Bartimaeus--a man blind from birth. He never saw a thing—not a sunset or a sunrise, not the faces of his parents, nor even the people who tossed coins into his cup as he begged on the side of the road.

There was also the leper. A man outcast by society, abandoned and shunned by his friends and family because they feared contracting the disease. This left him hurting and alone.

None of them knew what would happen when they reached Jesus, but they had a hope that He would indeed do something. Likewise, we are unable to see the future, but we can know that Jesus is still in the restoration business!

Perhaps you feel like Job from the Old Testament, overwhelmed with issues and struck with grief. Maybe you've searched high and low for something more in life but have come up empty again and again? Possibly you have even sought fulfillment in friends, or money, or pleasure, or career, yet feel emptier now than when you first began.

If so, let me give you some advice. You might not be able to see the future, but you can do what Charles Spurgeon did many years ago. Look to Jesus. He is the hope of the world.

CONSIDER
Like a sand castle struck by a thundering wave, everything seems to be falling apart and washing away in chapter 14. The pall of darkness is so great that no one sees that the greatest moment in human history is set to take place.

Indeed, when things look bad to our own earthly eyes, we often resign ourselves to failure, or loss, or disappointment. During these times, we forget that God's most significant work often comes from the deepest pains and worst moments.

As you read, consider how the Lord has used adverse events and issues to deepen you, to mature you, and to push you forward in life.

READ: MARK 14:43-72

INVEST
What happened to Jesus in the Garden?

How do the disciples react in verse 50?

How does the religious council treat Jesus?

In verses 66-72, what does Peter do?

If you did not know the end of the story, how do you think things are going to end for Jesus and His ministry?

As limited humans, we do not know the future. However, when difficult things and dark times invade our lives, why do we *not* need to despair?

In what ways have difficult things and dark times helped deepen and mature you?

PRAY
- Thank God for the negative things in your life that have helped you to grow
- Confess, if necessary, doing more complaining and despairing instead growing and trusting during those times
- Ask the Lord to develop, deepen, and mature you
- Ask the Lord to take the negative things in your life and use them to make you more like Him

TRAINING
Max Lucado once wrote that "in God's hands intended evil becomes eventual good," so repent of any despair and dedicate yourself to trusting God. Today,

we can read Mark 14 with a sense of hope because we know the end of the story.

Likewise, we can get through any situation because we know God is in control and He works out all things for the good of those who love Him and are called according to His purpose (Romans 8:28). Believe that "you got this" because God's got you!

MARK 15

START HERE

You know you are having a bad day when…

- Your horn sticks on the freeway behind a group of Hell's Angels
- You get to work and find a "60 Minutes" news team waiting in your office
- Your birthday cake collapses from the weight of the candles
- It costs more to fill up your car than it did to buy it
- The bird singing outside your window is a vulture
- You call your spouse and say that you would like to eat out tonight and when you get home there is a sandwich on the front porch
- Your kids start treating you the same way you treated your parents
- The health inspector condemns your office coffee maker
- The fortune teller offers to refund your money[35]

If any of the above "worst days" happen in your life, you could probably look back and laugh one day. Sometimes, however, there are events that no amount of time passing brings laughter. Such is the case with the awful events of Mark 15.

CONSIDER

For those living out Mark 15, it was the worst day of their lives. Their master and teacher was railroaded through an unfair and rigged trial, and then He is beaten, whipped, mocked, nailed to a cross, and mocked some more. Over a six-hour period, as the skies grow dark with thick, black clouds, the man who they had pinned their hopes on dies a painfully slow and suffocating death. Everything good that led up to that day was washed away by their tears. It must have seemed like it was all for nothing.

As you read, consider how you deal with life when all seems unfair, rigged, dark, and hopeless. Do those days tend to erase all the good that preceded, or do you cling to the good as you go through the bad?

READ: MARK 15

INVEST

In verse 15, how does Pilate seek to please people instead of doing what is right?

Have you been guilty of people pleasing over doing what is right? If so, what situations might cause this happen?

In verses 16-32, what does Jesus endure?

In verse 34, what does Jesus say?

Some might think that Jesus, like many of us, feels abandoned by God in difficulty, but that is not what is happening here. The Second Member of the Trinity takes our sin upon Himself. Our sin that God hates and wants to destroy. In His hatred for this sin, God rips Himself from His earthly communion with Christ. Experiencing this disunion for the first time since before there was time, Jesus cries out, "My God, my God, why have you forsaken me?" Understand, Jesus wept in the Garden, not for the coming pain of the nails, but because He knew our sin would cause God to disconnect from Him, so He could die as a sacrificial lamb. What can you do to honor such a sacrifice?

How do you handle things when everything seems to be going wrong? Do you remind yourself of God's love and sacrifice or struggle with feelings of despair?

In verse 43, it states that *Joseph took a risk.* He stood against his fellow Pharisees and proclaimed allegiance to Jesus. Are you more like Pilate who people pleased, or more like Joseph who went against his associates to stand for Jesus?

How do you think standing consistently for Jesus could help you when difficult times come into your life?

PRAY

- Thank Jesus for His willingness to be your sacrificial lamb
- Confess, if necessary, despairing more than trusting during difficult times
- Ask the Lord to make you a God-pleaser over a people pleaser
- Ask the Lord to fill you with His peace, hope, and joy whenever trials and struggles come into your life

TRAINING

To understand more about why Jesus would cry out to God, "My God, My God, why have you forsaken Me?" go to YouTube.com and type in *: Why did Jesus say, "My God, my God, why have you forsaken me?"* You will see a three minute, seven second video listed by Got Questions Ministries

MARK 16

START HERE

The great apostle Paul writes in Philippians 4:13 *I know how to live on almost nothing or with everything. I have learned the secret of living in every situation, whether it is with a full stomach or empty, with plenty or little. For I can do everything through Christ, who gives me strength.*

Paul says, "Here's the secret. It's all found in Christ." You can search down every other road you want, but you won't find joy there no matter how hard you look. You could look down the road of unbelief, pleasure, money, position, fame, career, etc., but you won't find it there. It is found in Christ alone—the same Christ, who for the joy set before Him, could endure unspeakable agony.

Again, there was nothing "happy" about the cross. There was nothing "happy" about Pontius Pilate who sentenced Jesus to death, the Roman soldiers who taunted, whipped, and beat Jesus, or the religious leaders who spit in Jesus' face and mocked Him.

There was nothing "happy" about the crown of thorns or the stick used to beat Jesus. There was nothing "happy" about dragging a cross up a hill, getting nailed to it, and slowly suffocating to death over a period of six hours.

These things could have destroyed Jesus, but Hebrews 12:2 tells us that, through it all, Jesus could endure because of the joy set before Him. A joy that could never be stolen away.

That same joy that was in Christ can be ours now through Christ. He defeated sin, death, and the grave, and He can defeat anything going on in our lives!

CONSIDER

As we enter Mark 16, hopelessness turns to hope, despair transforms into joy, and death becomes life. Jesus is alive! Sin, death, and the grave have been defeated! Christ arrives in power and everything changes.

Today, when we have days that seem hard and hopeless, we need to remember that Christ is alive, and He has the power to transform the worst situations into something unspeakably amazing. As you read, consider how much better life could be if you focused on those truths during difficult times.

READ: MARK 16

INVEST

In verse 7, what is the significance of the angel adding "including Peter"?

Peter denied Jesus three times, yet Jesus loved and forgave Him. How does this knowledge comfort you when you blow it?

What is our job according to verse 15?

How are you doing at fulfilling this job?

What more could you be doing?

Who do you know that needs the hope of the Gospel? List their names:

Where in your own life do you need to remind yourself about the hope of the Gospel?

PRAY

- Thank Jesus for His ability to transform the worst of things into amazing things
- Confess, if necessary, not focusing on the hope of the Gospel when things get tough
- Ask the Lord to fill you with His hope
- Ask the Lord to use you to make a difference in the lives of those around you

TRAINING

- Make sure to keep praying for the five people on your prayer card
- Seek opportunities to share the Gospel with at least one of those people

this week
- Adopt a missionary or country that you can be praying for each day
- Commit to praying for your church's pastor(s) and leadership team

LUKE 1:1-38

START HERE
"Luke's interest in people is undeniable. Much of the material unique to Luke's gospel involves Jesus' interactions with individuals, many of them on the fringes of "acceptable" society—sinners, women, and children among them. Like Matthew and Mark, Luke recorded the incident of a woman coming to pour perfume on Jesus' feet. But Luke was the only gospel writer to point out the fact known to all present that she was an immoral woman (Luke 7:37). In a similar way, we find in Luke alone the conversation between the robbers crucified alongside Jesus, one of them defending Jesus and receiving the promise of paradise. Luke's portrayal of Jesus reveals in our Lord a man come to minister and show compassion to all people, no matter their station in life."[36]

"The richness of Luke's portrayal of Jesus has profound implications for our relationship with God today. Jesus walks through Luke's gospel illustrating His deep and abiding care for people, regardless of what they have done or their status in society."[37]

CONSIDER
The book of Luke starts with two astounding stories of new life. First, an elderly, childless couple experience a miracle—a new child. Second, an impoverished teen with nothing to her name except simple faith in a mighty God will give birth to the Savior of the World.

As you read, consider what parts of your life need the breath of life blown into them.

READ: LUKE 1:1-38

INVEST
Why did it appear Zechariah and Elizabeth would never have children?

What did God do for this couple?

Where do you need God to do the miraculous in your life?

What did Gabriel tell Mary would happen in verses 31-33?

In Bible times, if a Jewish girl was unwed and pregnant, she would be an outcast at best or stoned to death at worst. Should she live, she would be a pariah and unable ever to marry. To survive, she would be reduced to begging or prostitution. Knowing all this, how does Mary respond in verse 38?

It took great faith for Mary to follow God's plan. How can a faith like Mary's help you as you wait for God to work the miraculous in your life?

God does the impossible two times in chapter 1. How does knowing that our God can do anything encourage you as you deal with potentially "impossible situations"?

PRAY
- Thank God for His ability to do the impossible and the miraculous
- Confess, if necessary, lacking a faith like Mary's
- Ask the Lord to deepen and expand your faith
- Ask the Lord to go to work in your life in miraculous ways

TRAINING
Consider the following ways to expand your faith in God:
- Practice counting your blessings. Thank God repeatedly throughout the day for things as simple as air, blue sky, trees, rain, a gentle breeze, water, food, etc.
- Be in a constant state of prayer. Talk to God throughout the day, using mini-sentence prayers. After doing something dumb, state, "Well, that wasn't too bright, was it, God?" After something breaks your way, give praise, "Thank You, God, for that blessing."
- Study the Word. Keep growing in wisdom and knowledge through the Scriptures
- Surround yourself with others who want to grow in faith. We become like those we spend time with, so spend your time with the right people
- Guard your heart. Don't allow Satan to lead you astray

LUKE 1:39-80

START HERE

Scottish minister Alexander Whyte was known for his uplifting prayers in the pulpit. He always found something for which to be grateful. One Sunday morning, the weather was so gloomy that one church member thought to himself, "Certainly the preacher won't think of anything for which to thank the Lord on a wretched day like this."

Much to his surprise, however, Whyte began by praying, "We thank Thee, O God, that it is not always like this."[38]

Indeed, there are always things to be thankful for. It just depends on how willing we are to look for them.

CONSIDER

Yesterday, we found Mary, Elizabeth, and Zechariah waiting on the Lord to do the impossible. Today, we will see them praising the Lord for the astonishing things that He does. Parents often teach their children to say, "Thank you" when someone does something nice for them. But, as children of God, how often do we take the time to praise and thank the Lord for everything He does in us, through us, and for us?

As you read, consider where you need answers to prayer and how diligent you are to praise God for the answers He provides.

READ: LUKE 1:39-80

INVEST

As we discussed yesterday, as an unwed, teenage girl, Mary could have easily been stoned to death. Yet, how does she praise the Lord in verses 46-55?

How well do you praise the Lord in the midst of confusing or difficult times?

What does Zechariah say in verses 78-79?

How can these words encourage you when times are tough?

Where do you need God to go to work right now?

How can you praise the Lord right now?

PRAY
- Thank God for at least five things. Be specific
- Confess, if necessary, being more whiney than thankful when things seem bleak
- Ask the Lord to go to work in your life
- Ask the Lord to fill you with a passion for praising His name

TRAINING
Both Mary and Zechariah expressed their praise and adoration for the Lord in chapter 1. Follow their lead and spend some time composing a letter to God, praising Him for what He has already done in your life, for what He is currently doing, and for what He has planned in the future.

LUKE 2

START HERE

In his book, *Christmas is not Your Birthday*, Mike Slaughter shares the story of a friend who writes, "The Christmas when my dad left our family was a very sad Christmas. I was about six years old. My aunts and extended family went out of their way to see we still had presents and a Christmas tree. While grateful for the gifts, it was not the presents under the tree that stuck in my mind. Instead, it was the lesson I learned…that God can and will help you get through the dark times in life."[39]

You do not need me to tell you that life gets messy. But in the midst of our mess, God shows up! No matter what you are going through or what you are struggling to overcome, God promises to show up. Just as God entered into a dark and imperfect world that first Christmas, so He will enter into our dark times as well.

CONSIDER

In chapter 1, Zechariah prophecies *the morning light from Heaven is about to break upon us to give light to those who sit in darkness.*[40] In chapter 2, that light arrives. However, this light does not descend majestically from Heaven, radiate brilliantly from a palace, or set a major city like Jerusalem aglow.

No, instead, the Light of World flickers in a dark hovel surrounded by animals. His first bed is a cow trough, and his first outfit consists of torn pieces of cloth. As you read, consider that no matter how bleak things may seem, the Light of the World is here.

READ: LUKE 2

INVEST

What does verse 7 say about Jesus' birth?

What do the angels say to the shepherds in verses 10-12?

If someone told you that the Messiah could be found in cow trough wearing strips of cloth, what would you think?

In spite of the angels' head-shaking announcement, the shepherds run to the stable. After meeting Jesus, what does verse 17 find them doing?

Who are you telling about the Savior who entered into our world?

What does Simeon say about Jesus in verse 32?

Who do you know that is in spiritual darkness and needs the Light of the World?

What can you do this week to tell at least one of those individuals about the Christ who came for them?

PRAY
- Thank Jesus for humbly entering this world
- Confess, if necessary, not pointing others to the Light of the World
- Ask the Lord to shine His light through you
- Ask the Lord to give you opportunities to shine His light into the people who still live in darkness

TRAINING
If you are struggling with the darkness in this world, consider a Christmas prayer written by Max Lucado after the Sandy Hook massacre:
Dear Jesus,

It's a good thing you were born at night. This world sure seems dark. I have a good eye for silver linings. But they seem dimmer lately...

The whole world seems on edge. Trigger-happy. Ticked off. We hear threats of chemical weapons and nuclear bombs. Are we one button-push away from annihilation?

Your world seems a bit darker this Christmas. But you were born in the dark, right? You came at night. The shepherds were nightshift workers. The Wise Men followed a star. Your first cries were heard in the shadows. To see your face, Mary and Joseph needed a candle flame. It was dark. Dark with Herod's jealousy. Dark with Roman oppression. Dark with poverty. Dark with violence.

Herod went on a rampage, killing babies. Joseph took you and your mom into Egypt. You were an immigrant before you were a Nazarene.

Oh, Lord Jesus, you entered the dark world of your day. Won't you enter ours? We are weary of bloodshed. We, like the wise men, are looking for a star. We, like the shepherds, are kneeling at a manger.

This Christmas, we ask you, heal us, help us, be born anew in us.

Hopefully,

Your Children[41]

LUKE 3

START HERE
There was a man who thought he was John the Baptist, so for public safety, he was committed. Put in a room with another person, he immediately began preaching to his new bunkmate. "I am John the Baptist! Jesus Christ has sent me to speak with you!"

The other instantly replied, "I most certainly did not send you!"

None of us are John the Baptist, but we all do have his job. Prepare the way for Christ.

CONSIDER
Prepare the way. That is the message of chapter 3. Jesus is set to begin His earthly ministry, and it was John the Baptist's role to set the stage, to get people thinking, to plant some seeds, and to open up some doors. Today, our role is very similar.

Jesus desires to work in the life of every single person on this planet, and we have the privilege of preparing the way. How we live, the words we use, the opportunities we grab, the attitudes we display, the choices we make, and so much more, all of it can be used to ready people for the work Christ wants to do in their lives.

As you read, consider if your life is being used to prepare those around you for an encounter with Christ.

READ: LUKE 3

INVEST
In verses 1-14, how did John the Baptist prepare the way for Jesus?

What does John say in verse 8?

Is your life proving to those around you that Jesus is both your Lord and your

Savior?

Where are you doing well? What needs improvement?

Don't think that because you have issues that the Lord can't use you. We must certainly be working on our weak areas, but those areas don't disqualify us from serving. Consider those in Jesus' lineage, as you did in the very first devotional from Matthew 1. Several of the those listed dealt with serious issues, yet, over time, their walk with the Lord deepened, and they were used in significant ways. How can this encourage you?

PRAY
- Thank God that He can forgive your past, bless your present, and use you to change lives in the future
- Confess, if necessary, using your past failures as an excuse not to serve God in the present
- Ask the Lord to use you to prepare the way for Him to enter the lives of all those around you
- Ask the Lord to make a mighty difference in and through you

TRAINING
- Look for ways to plant seeds in the lives of unbelieving friends, relatives, co-workers, classmates, and neighbors
- Offer to pray when someone shares a hurt or heartache
- Invite people over, or out, for a meal. Pray before you eat
- Keep your eyes open for where you can meet physical, emotional, or spiritual needs in those around you
- Watch your own words, actions, and attitudes. Frequently remind yourself that your home, your neighborhood, your workplace or school is your mission field

LUKE 4

START HERE

Have you ever been at a party where there's a box of powdered donut holes next to a vegetable tray? You know that you should eat the vegetables, but there's powdered donuts! The veggies, of course, are packed with vitamins and are low in fat, but there's powdered donuts!

These donuts, meanwhile, are filled with trans fats, saturated fats, and have absolutely no nutritional value, but, hey, they're powdered donuts!

You end up taking some vegetables and just two donut holes. After all, they are small. What harm could only two cause? And, let's remember, you have vegetables to balance out the donuts.

After eating the two donuts (in one second), you decide to head over to the food table again and grab another two. Just two. What's the big deal? How much harm could something so little cause? And they taste *so good.*

Later, someone else hears about the powdered donuts but cannot find them because the box is on your lap!

Temptation is much like those little, powdered donuts. Satan loves to remind us of all the good we are already doing (eating vegetables), as he puts something else into our hands. Not a big thing, mind you. Something small, something we don't think is so wrong, especially compared to the amount of good stuff in our life.

After he has us hooked, though, those small things start to get bigger. Soon the box is in our lap, and we need an intervention!

CONSIDER

Yesterday, we talked about being used by God to prepare the way for Jesus. Today, we will see that anyone interested in making a Kingdom difference in this world can count on Satan taking dead aim at them. Indeed, standing up for the Lord makes you an enemy of Satan.

Once you set yourself in opposition of the devil, he will tempt you, seek to make you ineffective, and distract you into apathy. As you read, consider how Satan may be attacking you. If you can't spot any signs of satanic attack, what might that tell you?

READ: LUKE 4

INVEST

How did Satan tempt Jesus in verses 1-11?

Each of the three times that the devil tempted Jesus, what did the Lord use to confront all the lies and half-truths?

What does this tell you about the need to study the Scriptures continually?

Jesus was not only tempted by Satan but taunted and hated by others. How do we see this in verses 28-30?

It is a guarantee that if you stand up for Christ, you will eventually be mocked, laughed at, misunderstood, and/or mistreated. Have you seen any of that in your life? If yes, how so?

If you can overcome the temptation of Satan and the taunting of others, you will have the privilege of seeing lives changed. How do we see this in verses 35-41?

Where can you make a difference this week?

PRAY

- Thank God for His power to help you overcome temptation
- Confess, if necessary, not working to make a difference in this world
- Ask the Lord to give you the strength to overcome the temptations of Satan and the taunts of the world
- Ask the Lord to deepen your understanding of Him and His Word

TRAINING

Need help memorizing Scripture, try these tips:

- Read the verse through several times thoughtfully, aloud or in a whisper. This will help you grasp the verse as a whole
- Work on saying the verse aloud as much as possible
- Think about how the verse applies to you and your daily circumstances
- Always include the topic and reference as part of the verse as you learn and review it
- Writing the verse out can be helpful. This act deepens the impression in your mind
- Review the verse immediately after learning it and repeat it frequently over the next few days[42]

LUKE 5

START HERE
In the late 1990s, I moved to Romania for one year. The plan was for me to begin a sports program at a K through eighth-grade school and also do likewise at a local boys' orphanage. Arriving at the school for the first time, I stood outside the building on the sidewalk. Within a couple of seconds, a student stuck his head out of a third-floor window and shouted, "You American?!?"

I looked up, and soon several faces were peering through closed windows or sticking out open ones. A chorus of "American?" swept across the third floor. Apparently, I stuck out, as they immediately pegged me as a foreigner!

1 Peter 2:11 states that Christians are foreigners in this world. This world is not our home, and our citizenship is in Heaven. That being the case, I have often wondered if people can peg me for being a Christian as easily as I was pegged for being an American that day in Romania.

How about you? Can people tell your citizenship is in Heaven?

CONSIDER
As we hit chapter 5, everything is coming together. Droves of people are coming to the Lord, being changed, and going out to share the Good News. Even with the nastiness of naysayers, the Kingdom is forcefully pushing forward.

As you read, consider how Jesus is changing you and how that change should be drawing those around you to want to know more.

READ: LUKE 5

INVEST
What does Peter say in verse 8?

Peter understood that work needed to be done in his life, but he missed the fact that the Lord could still use him while that work was going on. What does Jesus say to him in verse 10?

How did Peter (and James, John, and Andrew) respond?

How are you responding to Jesus' work in your life?

As we discussed in the devotional for Mark 1, it is ironic that the leper is instructed not to tell others about what Jesus had done (verse 14), and others were willing to break through someone's roof to get a friend to the Lord, yet, today, even with a command from Christ (review Matthew 28:18-20 and Mark 16:15), many are reluctant to share. How about you? To what lengths are you willing to go to share the Gospel?

What more could you be doing?

PRAY
- Thank God for the people who were willing to share the Gospel with you
- Confess, if necessary, not sharing the Good News as you should
- Ask the Lord to give you great boldness to share the Gospel
- Ask the Lord to work in your life that you might better reflect Him

TRAINING
Yesterday, in the TRAINING section, we looked at how to memorize Scripture. Consider memorizing the four Scriptures associated with the Romans Road so that you can quickly and easily share the Gospel with others
- Romans 3:23...*All have sinned and fallen short of the glory of God.* This means we are all sinners. We have all said, done, and thought wrong things. These wrong things are called sin
- Romans 6:23a...*For the wages of sin is death.* There is a penalty for sin, and it is death. All who sin are under this penalty. Since we all have sinned, we are all subject to death
- Romans 5:8... *But God demonstrates his own love for us in this: While we were still sinners, Christ died for us.* Christ was willing to take the penalty for our sins. Even though we were the ones who broke God's commandments, Jesus willingly became the sacrifice
- Romans 10:13...*Everyone who calls on the name of the Lord will be*

saved. If you recognize that you are a sinner who deserves the death penalty, but understand that Jesus took that penalty for you, then call out to the Lord in faith. Believe He died for you and now lives again, having defeated sin, death, and the grave

LUKE 6

START HERE

In 2017, a man bought a used car. Opening up the glove compartment for the first time, he found a list of twenty-two rules that a girl had apparently typed up for her boyfriend. The new owner of the vehicle found the list so insane that he posted a picture of it on Twitter. The post quickly went viral.

Check out some "highlights" from this list:
- You are NOT to have a single girls' phone number
- You are NOT to follow them on any social media (including Instagram, Snapchat, and Twitter)
- You are NOT to hang out with your friends more than two times a week
- You are NOT to look at a single girl
- If girls come up to you at any place or anytime, you are to WALK away
- You are NOT to get mad at me about a single thing ever again
- I am allowed to do a phone check when EVER I please
- You are NOT to ditch me for your friends
- We are to go on a legit date once every two weeks at least
- If I say jump, you say "how high princess"
- You are to make sure you tell me you love me once a day at least, so I know you're not messing around
- You are to NEVER take longer than 10 mins to text me back.[43]

I'm no relationship expert, but what the what! I don't think this young lady is going to keep her man for long! Rules-based dating doesn't usually work out too well.

The same holds true with our faith. When it comes to God, it cannot be about rules. It has to be about a relationship.

CONSIDER

Rules versus Relationship. Following commands versus following Christ. These contrasting views have been in a tug-of-war since the beginning of Christianity.

Sadly, many believe that the heart of Christianity I s following a list of do's and don'ts. Sure, there are commands, rules, and expectations that God requires us to obey, but the heart of Christianity is to be molded into the image of Christ, to love the Lord with our heart, soul, mind, and strength.

We should sincerely desire obedience, but not because we need to follow the rules. No, we should desire obedience because it honors the One who gave so much for us.

As you read, consider if you are contenting yourself with following some rules instead of diligently pursuing a life-altering relationship with the Lord.

READ: LUKE 6

INVEST
The Pharisees and other religious leaders focused solely on rules. In the process, they missed the Messiah right in front of them (verses 1-11). Do you tend to focus on commands over Christ? (i.e., "Did I do this? Did I stay away from that?" over "Am I more passionate about pursuing Christ today than I was yesterday?")

The heart of Christianity is found in verse 40. How are you doing at becoming more like Christ in speech, life, love, faith, and purity?

Sometimes we view Christianity as "Did I read my Bible? Did I pray? Did I refrain from cursing and having a bad attitude?" etc. Those things are important, but, frankly, you can accomplish them in your own strength without any need for God. However, loving your enemies, denying self, forgiving offenses, seeking purity, and more can only be done in God's strength as we rely on Him each moment of each day. How are you doing at relying on the Lord each moment of the day?

Where do you need work?

What can help you become more like Christ?

Are you doing these things? If not, when will you start?

PRAY
- Thank God for His Son, Jesus Christ
- Confess, if necessary, not working to be molded into His image
- Ask the Lord to mold you into the image of His Son, Jesus
- Ask the Lord to surround you with people who will encourage you to build your relationship with Christ

TRAINING
Here are a few ideas to help you shift from doing to being and from living for Christ to living like Christ:
- Pray and work. Do your work with an ear tuned to the voice of God. When you combine prayer and action, even trivial tasks can be ways to honor the Lord
- Play for an Audience of One. Seek the background rather than public accolades so that you will desire to please God rather than impress people
- Monitor your temptations as they arise (the lust of the flesh, the lust of the eye, the pride of life) and turn these moments into opportunities to focus on Jesus. We do not overcome sin by trying to avoid it, but by focusing on Jesus
- Experiment with prayer. For instance, try praying for strangers you see while you are walking, waiting in line, or driving. Ask the Lord to direct your prayers and listen for His promptings. Reach beyond your own concerns and become a channel of God's grace and mercy to others
- Develop an eye that looks for God's beauty and handiwork in nature. Learn to savor the wonders of the created order, since they point beyond themselves to the awesomeness of the Creator[44]

LUKE 7

START HERE

By the time he was nineteen, G. Campbell Morgan had already enjoyed success as a preacher, but soon doubts attacked his soul. The writings of various scientists and agnostics disturbed him (e.g., Charles Darwin, John Tyndall, Thomas Huxley, and Herbert Spencer).

As he read their books and listened to debates, Morgan became more and more perplexed. What did he do? He canceled all preaching engagements, put all the books in a cupboard and locked the door, and went to the bookstore and bought a new Bible. He said to himself, "I am no longer sure that this is what my father claims it to be—the Word of God. But of this I am sure. If it be the Word of God, and if I come to it with an unprejudiced and open mind, it will bring assurance to my soul of itself."

The result? "That Bible found me!" said Morgan. This new assurance enabled him to devote himself to the study and preaching of God's Word.[45]

CONSIDER

In chapter 6, we looked at rules versus relationship. Today, two new opponents enter the ring—faith and doubt. As we make our way through chapter 7, these two opposites will battle it out. Some adamantly refuse to accept Christ, while others choose to trust. But even among those who choose to trust, doubts and questions linger.

As you read, consider how firm your faith is and where you might have some doubts of your own.

READ: LUKE 7

INVEST

How do the Roman officer (verses 1-10) and the sinful woman (verses 36-39) show great faith?

How does John the Baptist show doubt in verses 18-20?

How do the Pharisees (verse 30) and Simon (verses 36-39) show little to no belief at all?

Where do you fall? Are you more like the Centurion or Simon, the woman or the Pharisees?

Having some doubts is not wrong. Those doubts can show a desire to understand more fully. If you do have some doubts, where are you going for answers?

What can you do to strengthen your faith?

PRAY
- Thank Jesus for being worthy of all your faith, trust, and belief
- Confess, if necessary, any doubts that you might be having
- Ask the Lord to guide you to the right people who can assuage and answer those doubts
- Ask the Lord to deepen, grow, and mature your faith

TRAINING
Check out gotquestions.org. This website has over 550,000 answers to biblical and faith-based questions!

LUKE 8

START HERE

The word "awesome" has been around a long time in our culture. Other words have come along and worked to supplant it, but those words seem to fade away while "awesome" keeps hanging on.

Consider just some words that have been used for "awesome" over the last thirty years – the bomb, the bomb-diggity, crackalackin, ill, killer, boss, dirty, off the hook, off the chain, off the heezie, off the hizzle, epic, phat, rad, lit, redonkulous, righteous, sic, sic-nasty, slammin, stellar, fresh, stupid-fresh, sweet, tight, wizard, and all that and a bag of chips.

These words, along with many others, have come and gone, but awesome remains.
"That movie was awesome!"
"That roller coaster was awesome!"
"This new app is awesome!"
 "Doing my taxes this year was awesome!" Okay, maybe not that one.

Regardless of how many things we label as awesome, there is no awesomeness compared to the awesomeness of God. In the Bible, the Hebrew word for "awesome" is used over three hundred and seventy times in the Old Testament—and the majority of the time, it is referring to God.

Again and again, the Bible wants to emphasize there is only one that is the bomb or the boss. There is only one that is off the hizzle and redonkulous. There is only one that is sic, righteous, and stupid-fresh. There is only one that is awesome—the Lord God Almighty.

Nevertheless, how often to do we trade the awesomeness of God for such little things—movies, TV shows, the internet, our phones, sports, bands, hobbies, etc. We've convinced ourselves that these little things are awesome as well, and so we never think about the poor trade that we've made.

CONSIDER

Movies, TV shows, websites, bands, actors, tech gadgets, sports' stars, or whatever else, won't be there for you when you're battling depression, dealing with cancer, struggling with sin, feeling alone, fighting pain, or looking for answers. But there is One who will be there for you through all of that and more. (You will meet Him today in your reading!)

Don't trade Him away for lesser things—seek to experience just how awesome the Lord is. If you do, then you just might understand what this word "awesome" really, truly means.

As you read, consider how often you contemplate the awesomeness of a God who would take on flesh and enter into our broken world.

READ: LUKE 8

INVEST
What is the meaning of each of the four seeds?

Which seed most resembles your life right now?

If you didn't answer "definitely the fourth one," what changes must you make?

To show the disciples (and the rest of us) that fully investing in Him is totally worth it, Jesus takes the twelve through a series of events in verses 22-56. In verses 22-25, how does Jesus show His protective power?

In verses 26-39, how does Jesus show His power to deal with the most difficult of people or situations?

In verses 40-56, how does Jesus show His power to heal, bless, and transform?

How should understanding what Jesus can offer the world inspire you to share Him with others?

How should knowing all that you can have in Christ cause you to forsake the world and grab hold of Him with both hands?

PRAY

- Thank Jesus for His power to protect, provide, bless, heal, and transform
- Confess, if necessary, not making a difference in this world for Christ
- Ask the Lord to grant you opportunities to share Him with others
- Ask the Lord to help you find satisfaction and fulfillment in Him and not in the world

TRAINING

As we discussed in Mark 12, the answer to more fulfillment, deeper satisfaction, and enduring purpose is not found in things, no matter how many of those things you may happen to have. The answer is found in Christ.

So how are things going for you? If you seem to be continually coming up empty, perhaps it is because you have not been searching for more in Christ. If your life is not infused with purpose, perhaps it is because you have been dipping your bucket into the wrong well. If so, it's time to start swimming in the vast ocean of God's grace, Christ's love, and the Spirit's infilling.

Understand. When you seek more in Christ, He makes more out of you!

Your next step is to look to Christ, to seek more of Him, and to understand His will for you right now. Fall on your knees, crawl into the lap of your Heavenly Father, and cry out, "Lord, give me more of your Son. Fill me with more of Christ. Begin to use me to do more than I ever thought possible."

LUKE 9:1-45

START HERE

Two men, John Ford and Bob Smith, were applying for the same engineering job. Since both applicants had the same qualifications, management decided to give them each a ten question proficiency test.

Upon completion of the test, John and Bob each only missed one of the questions. Yet, John got the job. A decision that made Bob quite upset.

"Why did you give the other guy the job? We both have the same qualifications, and both got nine out of ten questions correct."

"Well, Mr. Smith," the manager started. "We made our decision not on the correct answers, but on the question you missed."

"And just how would one incorrect answer be better than the other?"

"Simple," the manager began again. "For question five, Mr. Ford put down 'I don't know,' and you put down 'Neither do I.'"

Thankfully, the Lord does not require proficiency tests to serve in the Kingdom. If so, I think many of us might be in trouble.

CONSIDER

"Look at me! Look what I can do!" Phrases like that don't fit too well in the Kingdom of God. Life in the Kingdom is about what God can do through us, not what we can do on our own. Kingdom living involves your availability, not your ability. It's not telling God, "Look at all I have to offer." No, it's telling God, "Here I am, Lord. Use me to do Your will."

It's so easy to get caught up in the dreaded, "I'm not qualified" syndrome. But our qualifications mean very little to God. The Lord doesn't take resumes, keep the best ones, and then chuck the rest. God doesn't sift through S.A.T. scores and report cards looking for the A-students. God doesn't look up our bank statements seeking the wealthiest people to advance His cause.

Instead, He pushes aside everything the world calls important, peers right into our hearts, and asks just one question—Are you willing?

As you read, consider how you view your role in God's Kingdom.

READ: LUKE 9:1-45

INVEST

Jesus sent out the twelve to make a difference in the Father's name. However, the disciples returned, exclaiming, "Jesus, You won't believe all *we* did" (verse 10). This is quite a different statement than, "Wow! You won't believe all that God did through us!" What does this tell you about the disciples' mindset?

Because of this upside down mindset, Jesus has some things planned (see John 6:6). It starts with needing to feed five thousand men (plus women and children). What did Jesus say to the twelve in verse 13?

How do the "self-sufficient" disciples respond in the same verse?

What lesson did the disciples hopefully learn after verses 14-17?

What does Jesus say in verses 23-25 to make it clear that life is not about us and what we can do?

How do you tend to view Kingdom work? Is it what you can do or what God can do through you?

Have you surrendered yourself over to God's use? What might be holding you back?

What would your life look like if you turned from your selfish ways, took up your cross, and followed Christ? Would it look any different than it does right now? Why or why not?

PRAY

- Thank God for all that He can accomplish through you
- Confess, if necessary, a "more about me than God" attitude
- Ask the Lord to use you to make a fantastic difference in this world
- Give yourself over to God, put yourself in His hands, and allow Him to lead you wherever He wants you to go

TRAINING

Consider the following questions:

- Are you willing to stand up for Christ even when no one else does? Are you willing to walk forward with Christ, even if everyone else is walking backward?
- Are you willing to die to yourself, so that you can live for Christ? Are you willing to care more about what will save the most people and help them grow in Christ than you care about your own wants and desires for your life or your church?
- Are you willing to let Christ interfere with your life for God's glory and the benefit of a desperately needy world?
- Are you willing to do all these things *not* because you think it is a duty, *not* because you believe it is in the rule book, *not* because it will make you look holy or good, *not* for any of that, but because Christ is worth it, and there is a lost and hurting world heading to Hell?

LUKE 9:46-10:24

START HERE

A husband and wife were involved in a petty argument, with both unwilling to admit they might be wrong. In an attempt to reconcile, the wife said, "I'll admit I'm wrong if you'll admit I'm right." The husband agreed and, being a gentleman, insisted she go first.

"I'm wrong," the wife acknowledged.

"You're right!" the husband replied.

We humans usually don't like to admit it when we are wrong. However, humility and honesty are keys to the Christian life. How are you doing with those "H" words?

CONSIDER

Most people, when they blow it, usually try extra hard to make up for it. The disciples, as we saw yesterday, discovered that they were not as great as they thought they were. (Though that still doesn't stop them from arguing about it in verses 9:46-48!) Caught again in foolish behavior, the twelve redouble their efforts…only to fail! Then fail again!

When we mess up, instead of going into overdrive covering things up in an attempt to look good, it is vital that we humble ourselves, apologize, and use the experience to help us grow. As you read, consider how you handle things after you blow it.

READ: LUKE 9:46-10:24

INVEST

When caught being prideful again (9:46-48), how did the disciples try to look good in verses 9:49-50 and 9:51-56?

How did that go for them?

After you blow it, how do you usually handle it?

Why is it important to humble yourself instead of trying harder to look good?

In verses 10:13-15, Jesus condemns the pride of several cities. How was this a message to His disciples (and us) as well?

What are some things that keep people from admitting their faults?

If you have a difficult time humbling yourself and apologizing after messing up, what can help you mature in this area?

PRAY
- Thank God for His willingness to forgive you after sinning
- Confess, if necessary, going into "cover up" mode after blowing it instead of humbling yourself and seeking forgiveness
- Ask the Lord to give you a humble and contrite spirit
- Give to the Lord any specific sins you may be covering up right now

TRAINING
We only improve on the things we practice. With that in mind, consider the following things you can do to practice humility:
- Avoid taking credit
- Praise others
- Help others succeed
- Admit your mistakes
- Learn from others
- Go last
- Serve someone[46]

LUKE 10:25-11:13

START HERE

I don't know how it was with your group of friends in high school. But when I was in high school, my group of friends did not particularly care for the more "studious" amongst us—i.e., those bookworms who threw off the curve.

In eleventh grade, I had a class that, on paper, was called "Chemistry." In reality, it should have been labeled "A Peak into the Seventh Level of Hell." The teacher, clearly knowing the class would be mind-bogglingly torturous, stated he would grade all tests on a curve. The highest grade in the class would receive a 100%, and the rest would rise commensurately. In other words, if the highest grade achieved was a 90%, it would rise ten percentage points, and so would all the rest of the scores.

This gracious grading system seemed to offer all the "regular schleps" a ray of hope (or a drop of water to quench our tongues in the flames). *However,* one annoyingly studious young lady always seemed to get at least a 98%, giving the rest of us, at most, a two-point bump! Evil, just pure evil.

Now that I am older, I realize that this young lady was right. Learning and studying are crucial to life, especially for the Christian. So, Julie, a belated thanks for the lesson. And any notes that may or may not have been shoved into a crack in your locker…let's just all move on.

CONSIDER

Jesus is always working to teach His people. This means we should always be walking around with our eyes and ears wide open so that we don't miss a single teachable moment.

In our Scripture for today, Jesus is working to teach all those around Him about love, about priorities, and about the power of prayer. Some were ready to learn; others not so much.

As you read, consider how good a student you are, especially when it comes to Christianity 101.

READ: LUKE 10:25-11:13

INVEST
Samaritans and Jews, in Bible times, generally despised each other. Understanding this dynamic, what was Jesus trying to teach about loving your neighbor in verses 30-37?

It is easy to love people who love you back, but how well do you love those who don't like you at all?

What do you still need to learn in this area?

What did Jesus tell a distracted Martha in verses 41-42?

Do you tend to get distracted from eternal matters by the temporary stuff of this world like movies, internet, TV, hobbies, sports, etc.?

What do you still need to learn in this area?

In verses 11:5-10, Jesus urges us to be persistent in prayer, even if it takes weeks, months, or years for answers. Would you say that you are someone who is persistent in prayer? Why or why not?

What do you still need to learn in this area?

PRAY
- Thank the Lord for always working to teach, instruct, and grow you
- Confess, if necessary, not being the student of Jesus that you should be
- Ask the Lord to help you learn all the lessons He wishes to teach you
- Ask the Lord to throw open your eyes and ears, so you won't miss a single thing He is doing around you

TRAINING

Looking to grow in your knowledge and understanding of God and His Word, consider the following:

- Attend a Bible-believing church every week
- Join a Christian small group
- Read the Bible every single day
- Pray continually
- Spend time worshipping the Lord and praising His name each day
- Find ways to serve in a ministry on a consistent basis
- Share the Gospel with others

LUKE 11:14-54

START HERE

You don't learn anything the second time you're kicked by a mule.

Some people, it seems, never learn. Take, for example, two buddies sitting in a pub watching the eleven-o'clock news. A story flashed on the screen about a man threatening to jump from the twentieth floor of a downtown building, causing one friend to turn to the other, "I'll bet you dinner the guy doesn't jump."

"It's a bet," agreed his buddy.

A few minutes later, the man on the ledge jumped. "I guess I'm buying dinner."

"No, forget, it," friend number two began. "I saw him jump earlier on the six-o'clock news."

"Me too! But I didn't think he'd do it again!"

Life is full of lessons. It all comes down to whether or not we want to learn.

CONSIDER

In our last devotion, we stressed the need for Christians to be students who desire to learn and grow. Today, we'll encounter many who simply are not interested in learning. Instead of being filled with a yearning to grow, these people are filled with pride and stubbornness.

As you read, consider how willing you are to learn from the Scriptures, from the Spirit, from your pastors, and from others who teach the ways of God.

READ: LUKE 11:14-54

INVEST

In verses 14-16, what are some negative people in the crowd thinking about Jesus?

What does Jesus say to the religious leaders in verses 39-52?

What makes people "blessed" according to Jesus in verse 28?

Are you diligent about studying God's Word and putting it into practice?

Where do you need improvement in this area?

What does Jesus say in verse 36?

Do you have any "dark corners" that need to be dealt with?

If so, when will you deal with them?

PRAY
- Thank God for all He desires to do in, with, and through you
- Confess, if necessary, not studying the Word and/or not putting it into practice
- Ask the Lord to show you how to apply His Word to your life
- Ask the Lord to work on any "dark corners" you may have

TRAINING
Make sure you are putting into practice some of the things we've discussed:
- Have you made a prayer card and filled it with the names of five unsaved people that you know?
- Are you praying over that list on a daily basis, asking the Lord to open their hearts to His message and to give you opportunities to share the Gospel?
- Are you consistently doing devotions each day?
- Are you attending church each week?
- Have you found a ministry to serve in consistently?
- Do you have an accountability partner who can encourage you?

LUKE 12

START HERE

I must confess that I have many problems. I don't know exactly how many problems though, because being bad at math is one of them.

I do tend to hide my problems. I usually walk around like I am fine, but, deep down, inside my shoe, there is a sock that is falling off. Worse than that, sometimes I spend hours just wishing my teeth were as white as my legs. True, some days I amaze myself, but most days I find myself looking for my phone while talking on it.

I haven't been able to get up without sound effects for years. And don't get me started on my attention deficit disorder, and what's wrong with pie anyway?

Problems. All of us have them. The question is, will we allow the Lord to deal with them?

CONSIDER

In chapter 12, Jesus seeks to tackle the unholy trinity of hypocrisy, greed, and worry. These three things will keep us from fully living out our faith and fulfilling our responsibilities as God's children.

Hypocrisy, acting outwardly one way while inwardly being something else, will be the first thing the Lord attacks. We might be able to fool others with our masks, but we can never fool God. He knows exactly what's going on at all times.

Secondly, Jesus will lambast greed—that is a focus on worldly things over the things of God. Most of us probably would not consider ourselves to be "greedy," yet are we continually sidetracked from Kingdom pursuits by our quest for more stuff, the newest gizmos, the trendiest fads, the latest in must-see TV, etc.?

Finally, the Lord goes after worry—the one sin no one ever thinks of as sin. But when we worry, we display a fundamental lack of faith and trust in God's goodness and provision. Further, worry cripples our witness as few people can serve the Lord effectively while obsessing over issues.

As you read, consider where hypocrisy, greed, or worry might have a hold of you.

READ: LUKE 12

INVEST

What does Jesus say about hypocrisy in verses 2-3?

How is this a good reminder that we may be able to fool others, but we are never fooling God?

What story does Jesus tell in verses 13-21 to combat greed?

What does the Lord specifically say in verse 21?

How does verse 34 tie in with verse 21?

As you look at an average week, how much time are you investing in your relationship with God compared to worldly pursuits?

What does Jesus say about worry in verses 22-28?

Do you tend to be a worrier?

What things can you do to help build your faith and trust?

Verse 31 really strikes at the heart of Christianity. What does it say?

How are you doing at this? What is going well? What needs some improvement?

PRAY

- Thank God that your faith and trust in Him is never misplaced
- Confess, if necessary, struggling with hypocrisy, greed, and/or worry
- Ask the Lord to give you a desire to seek first the Kingdom of God
- Ask the Lord to deepen your faith and trust in Him

TRAINING

- Allow the Lord to examine every part of your life
- Hold up the mirror, be humble, and let God look at every part of your heart, mind, and life

LUKE 13

START HERE
Our culture is pretty good at coming up with "solutions" to change how we look on the outside. Companies will even promise that changing the outside will indeed affect the inside. "You want to have more confidence? Lose fifty pounds. Whiten your teeth. Remove hair if you have too much; put hair on your head if you have too little. Do these things, and then you'll have confidence, get the girl, land the guy, be happy…"

Our culture says the key to contentment and satisfaction is changing your outside, but nothing could be further from the truth. Yet, please don't misunderstand what I am saying. There is nothing wrong with working on your outward appearance.

What's wrong is thinking that changing the outside is the answer to an improved life. Paint and detail work on a car won't fix problems under the hood, and it won't work on us either. Don't buy the lie that a little weight loss, a bit more hair on the head, a lot less hair on the back (ugh), some nicer teeth, etc. is going to fill the emptiness in your life, lessen stress and anxiety, and make everything alright. Not. Gonna. Happen.

What we need is a change from the inside out, and that only happens one way. That way is not through surgery, a weight loss plan, great dentistry, or some self-improvement plan. It can only happen through a relationship with Jesus Christ—one where He gets into your life and begins a radical work *inside* you.

CONSIDER
Where do you stand in your relationship with the Lord? That is the focal question of chapter 13, so it is no coincidence that, within this chapter, we find a woman who has been bent double for more than eighteen years.

Many are in such condition spiritually. The problem is, unlike the woman, most are unaware. As you read, consider where you stand with the Lord. Are you standing tall, or are you in need of some intervention?

READ: LUKE 13

INVEST

In verses 1-5, Jesus basically says, "When you hear that people have died, you probably believe that God has punished them for something. But what you should be thinking is, 'Wow! Any day might be my last. How is my relationship with the Lord? Will I be ready to meet Him when my day comes?'" With that in mind, how is your relationship with God?

In verses 6-9, Jesus uses a parable to remind us that God is patient and desires to see us grow and produce fruit. However, His patience does not last forever. Thinking about that, where do you need work and improvement in your Christian life?

What does Jesus say in verse 24?

This verse confuses some because it seems like Jesus is saying we must "work" to be saved. However, please understand that Jesus did all the work necessary for salvation through the cross. We do not "work" to be saved, but there is "work" to be done on our end to grow and mature—removing sin, denying self, seeking first the Kingdom, and more. How are you doing with that "work"?

What is Jesus trying to convey in verses 25-27?

Praying a "prayer of salvation" one time, going to church regularly, tithing, or even doing this devotional daily does not save you from sin. Many are fooled into thinking they are standing straight and secure because they do these things. The key to having a right standing with God, however, is found in chapter 14 (put God first, deny self, and pick up your cross). Knowing this, would you say that you are standing tall in God's eyes?

In verses 34-35, how do we see Jesus' desire for all to come to Him for transformation?

How can this knowledge encourage you when you blow it?

PRAY

- Thank Jesus for offering salvation through His death on the cross
- Confess, if necessary, thinking you are standing strong when perhaps you are not
- Ask the Lord to breathe His breath of life into your heart, mind, and soul
- Ask the Lord to help you deny yourself, pick up your cross, and follow Him

TRAINING

Take a few moments for spiritual examination. Ask yourself the questions below to see where you are standing straight and what areas may need some work.

- What disappointments has God allowed in my life? How have these affected my love for him?
- In what ways do I least reflect the image and likeness of God?
- How can I better order my life so that I preserve time for God and for other relationships God has entrusted to me?
- With whom am I most angry and frustrated at this time? Is there someone with whom I am looking to get even? Am I harboring resentment in my heart?
- In what ways have I given into lust?
- How can I take less and give more?
- Am I faithful with what God has entrusted to me—time, talents, treasures?
- What are the greatest desires of my heart right now? How do these relate to God's purpose for my life?[47]

LUKE 14

START HERE

A man received a promotion to the position of vice president of the company for which he worked. The new job quickly went to his head, and for weeks on end, he bragged to anyone and everyone that he was now a VP.

His bragging came to an abrupt halt when his wife, so embarrassed by his behavior, said, "Listen, Bob, it's not that big a deal. These days everyone's a vice president. Why they even have a vice president of peas down at the supermarket!"

Somewhat deflated, Bob headed down to the local supermarket to find out if this was true. "Can I speak to the vice president of peas please?" he asked the first employee he could find.

"Of fresh or frozen?" came the reply.[48]

Bob is not the only one who needs to remember that we all need to swallow our pride. Don't worry. It's not fattening.

CONSIDER

Humility. We all like to think that we have it. In reality, however, few of us actually do. Self and pride, it seems, are more fitting for the average human. Yet, the Christian life is about transformation—Pride metamorphosizing into humility and self-centeredness dissolving into other-centeredness.

As you read, consider if these transformations are occurring in you.

READ: LUKE 14

INVEST

What did Jesus notice in verse 7?

After noticing this, what advice does Jesus give in verses 8-10?

Do you tend to want to be first, to get the best seat, to have others see you getting accolades, etc.? If so, what might this tell you?

In verses 16-24, Jesus tells a parable about the Kingdom of God. A man (representing the Lord) invites everyone to enjoy His provision, but most refuse. They are too busy fulfilling their own plans, living out their own dreams, and chasing after their own desires. How about you? On a scale of one to ten, with one being "not at all" and ten being "all in," rate how well you have set aside your plans, dreams, and desires to live out God's call on your life. Explain your rating:

If it wasn't clear before, Jesus makes what it means to follow Him abundantly obvious in verses 26, 27, and 33. What does He say in those verses?

In verses 26-35, Jesus is essentially asking three questions—Do you understand what following Me will cost? Are you willing to pay the price? And do you recognize who is in charge? How do you answer those three questions?

Where might you need work?

PRAY
- Thank God for His transformative power
- Confess, if necessary, following your own plans, dreams, and desires over God's plans, dreams, and desires
- Ask the Lord to guide you clearly down the path He has for you
- Ask the Lord to use you in a mighty way to build His kingdom

TRAINING
- Review verses 26-35
- Spend time looking at those three questions Jesus is really asking in those verses—Do you understand what following Me will cost? Are you willing to pay the price? And do you recognize who is in charge?

LUKE 15

START HERE
There, but for the grace of God, go I.

Perhaps you have heard this phrase before. While not 100% verifiable, some historians believe that the above phrase was used regularly by the sixteenth-century evangelical preacher John Bradford. Regularly seeing prisoners sent to jail or the scaffold (to be hung), he would remark, "There, but for the grace of God, goes John Bradford."[49]

Unfortunately, in 1555, John would get his turn, burned at the stake for preaching Christ during the reign of "Bloody Mary." Condemned to die along with a young man named John Leaf, he turned to Leaf as the flames began to build, and said, "Be of good comfort brother; for we shall have a merry supper with the Lord this night!"[50]

CONSIDER
In the previous devotion, we looked at humility. Part of humility is recognizing that without Jesus we would be blind, but with Him, we can see. Without Jesus we would be lost, but with Him, we have our bearings. Without Jesus we would be spiritually dead, but with Him, there is eternal life.

Understanding these things allows us to humbly reach out to the hurting, the broken, the drunk, the prostitute, the prisoner, the homosexual, and more. Instead of pointing a condescending finger or looking down our noses at them, we realize that "There, but for the grace of God, go I."

As you read, consider if you truly understand exactly where you would be without Jesus in your life.

READ: LUKE 15

INVEST
How do verses 3-10 illustrate God's pursuit of lost people?

In verses 11-24, how does the youngest son represent all of us?

In those same verses, how do we see God in the boy's father?

In verses 25-30, how does the oldest son react to his brother's return?

How do you think you would feel if you saw God blessing the person you least liked in this world? Would you be happy, or would you be like the oldest son?

What might your answer tell you about where your heart is?

PRAY
- Thank God for His forgiveness and restoration
- Confess, if necessary, being like the oldest son
- Ask the Lord to help you see lost, hurting, and broken people as He does
- Ask the Lord to give you opportunities to work in the lives of those people

TRAINING
- Make a list of three to five people that you don't particularly care for
- Dedicate to daily pray for these people, asking the Lord to bless them

LUKE 16

START HERE

I am a child of the 1980s. I grew up in an era that considered a twenty-five inch picture tube a "big screen" TV. I had a boom-box, top-loading VCR, cassette tapes, mullet, Rubik's cube, and Mattel's Intellivision.

One Christmas, not too long ago, I got a "retro-Intellivision" (a controller with twenty-five Intellivision games built into it). I was excited to relive my childhood by playing *Astrosmash* and *Major League Baseball*. When I sat down to play, my son took one look at the graphics and laughed his head off. He couldn't believe anyone would want to play a game with such poor graphics. Yet, when I was a kid, I thought the graphics were amazing!

Funny, how things change over time. As each fad comes in with a bang and goes out with a whimper, we are continually reminded that the things of this world are so very temporary. Everything comes and goes. Of course, a few things come and go and then come back again—like bellbottoms. I was glad to see them go the first time, but then they came back again. (Whose idea was this anyway? I didn't get any emails about it.)

The stuff of the world never endures over the long-haul. It will come and go, leaving us just as we were when it arrived (only now a bit poorer). Don't get me wrong. If you want a plasma screen, an I-pod, a blue-ray player, the new Xbox (whichever one it is now), or even a "Vote for Pedro" shirt, that is fine. Just understand that the best stuff can do for you is offer temporary fixes. It can never give you permanent happiness, hope, love, joy, peace, wisdom, direction, etc.

The danger comes when you live for the temporary or for what the culture says is cool. Doing so causes you to flit from one thing to another in an effort to keep up with what's new. When it is all said and done, you are just as unfulfilled as when it all began--except now your home and life are filled with tired, old stuff that bores you.

There is a better way. Jesus offers it to us. Instead of living for more from the culture, we live for more of Him. Instead of surrendering time, money, and effort to temporary fads and quick-fixes, we surrender our lives to Him.

CONSIDER

Things, stuff, possessions, property—we spend a lifetime accumulating all of these things. In the end, though, none of it will go with us into eternity. And, really, if we are honest, we probably don't want it to anyway because it all has begun to bore, rust, go out of style, stop trending…wait, did I mention all of this already?

All those things that we work so hard to buy and then try so desperately to hold on to were not meant solely for our personal enjoyment. Everything we have should be used to glorify God and benefit others. When we hold onto to it all for ourselves, we end up more selfish and materialistic while the world ends up less blessed and less encouraged. Further, as we become more self-absorbed, God stops looking our way and turns to others who will properly use what they've been given.

As you read, consider how caught up in your stuff you might be.

READ: LUKE 16

INVEST

In verses 1-9, Jesus tells a story about a conniving servant who uses his abilities and his resources to benefit others and build relationships illegally. From that, Jesus points out that if a manipulative man will do that to save himself from a life of begging, how much more should we seek to use our resources to save others from an eternity in Hell? With this in mind, how are you using what God has blessed you with?

What is Jesus saying in verses 10-13?

Have you been faithful in using your time, talents, and resources to build God's Kingdom? If not, what needs to change?

In verses 19-31, what did all the rich man's wealth get him in the end?

How does this remind you of what Jesus said in verse 12:21?

170

Before it is too late for all those around you, how can you help them see that it is Jesus they need most, not stuff or money?

In verse 15, Jesus notes that the world often honors what God detests. Many things that distract us from time building the Kingdom (movies, music, video games, the internet) likely disgust God. Some of those things may win Game of the Year, Oscars, Emmys, Grammys, etc., yet their content issues and message deeply grieve the heart of God. Would you say you're distracted by things that the world applauds but God detests?

If so, what might need to change?

PRAY
- Thank God for being all that you need to be truly satisfied
- Confess, if necessary, being distracted by the things of this world (even things that God despises)
- Ask the Lord to provide you with opportunities to use your abilities and resources to build His Kingdom
- Ask the Lord to remove anything from your life that displeases Him

TRAINING
- Review how you spend your time. Is any of it wasted with trivial pursuits or with things that the Lord disapproves?
- Look through your movie, music, and video game collections. What among those things might have content issues—foul language, gore, blasphemy, sexual situations, excessive violence?
- How do you spend your money? Are you often getting new stuff, or are you using your money to build the Kingdom?
- Look through your home and storage areas. What do you have that could serve Kingdom purposes?

LUKE 17

START HERE
The boss of a big company needed to call one of his employees about an urgent problem with one of the central computers. He dialed the employee's home phone number and was greeted with a child's whispered, "Hello?"

Feeling put out at the inconvenience of having to talk to a youngster, the boss asked, "Is your Daddy home?"

"Yes," breathed the small voice.

"May I talk with him?" the man asked. To the surprise of the boss, the small voice whispered, "No." Wanting to talk with an adult, the boss asked, "Is your Mommy there?"

"Yes", came the answer.

"May I talk with her?"

Again, the hushed little voice replied, "No."

Knowing that it was not likely that a young child would be left home alone, the boss decided he would leave a message with the person who should be there watching over the child. "Is there anyone there besides you?"

"Yes," the child murmured, "a policeman."

Wondering what a cop would be doing at his employee's home, the boss asked, "May I speak with the policeman?"

"No, he's busy," said the child, still whispering.

"Busy doing what?"

"Talking to Daddy and Mommy and the Fireman", came a soft answer.

Growing concerned and even worried as he heard what sounded like a helicopter through the earpiece on the phone the boss asked, "What is that noise?"

"A hello-copper."

"What is going on there?" asked the boss, now alarmed.

"The search team just landed the hello-copper."

Alarmed, concerned, and more than just a little frustrated the boss asked, "What are they searching for?"

The young voice replied along with a muffled giggle, "Me!"[51]

CONSIDER
"Ready or not, here I come!"

These famous words that have started many a game of Hide-n-Seek will one day be used by Jesus. We don't know if it will be twenty minutes from now or twenty years from now, but one day the Lord will return. Without warning, the skies will open up. And, whether we are ready or not, the Lord will come and separate the world into two groups—those going to Heaven and those going to Hell.

As you read, consider how ready you are for Jesus' return and also how ready you are making those around you.

READ: LUKE 17

INVEST
The opposite of getting people ready to meet Jesus is leading them into temptation. What does the Lord say about this in verses 1 and 2?

Wow! Even though we also read these verses in Matthew 18, it is incredible to think that Jesus would prefer we drown over leading someone into temptation! How should such an understanding change how you act around others, how you dress, what you watch and listen to, your everyday conversations, etc.?

According to verse 3, what should we do if we see someone sinning?

Do you work to lovingly correct people who are making decisions that are moving them farther from the Lord, or do you tend to ignore such things and "not get involved"?

Why is "not getting involved" a bad idea?

Jesus reminds the people of the judgment that came during Noah's day and to Sodom. The Second Coming of the Lord will bring one last time of judgment. Are you ready?

What are you doing to stay ready? What are you doing to help others get, or stay, ready?

PRAY
- Thank Jesus for His promise to come again
- Confess, if necessary, not being ready for that return or not helping others get ready
- Ask the Lord to work in the lives of your friends, relatives, co-workers, classmates, and neighbors
- Ask the Lord to give you opportunities to work in their lives

TRAINING
- Continue praying for the five people you have listed on your prayer card
- Seek opportunities with these individuals to display Christ with your actions and share Christ with your words

LUKE 18

START HERE
Moist, blog, lugubrious, yolk, gurgle, phlegm, fetus, curd, smear, squirt, chunky, orifice, maggots, viscous, queasy, bulbous, pustule, fester, secrete, munch, clogged, vomit, jowls, dripping, roaches, mucus, slacks, and slurp.[52]

Is that my try at poetry? Thankfully, no. The words above are often on lists of the worst sounding terms in the English language. You may agree or disagree with the above list. However, I think most will agree that the three words we'll be looking at today are not pleasing to most of our ears.

CONSIDER
If you were to ask people what their least favorite words were, I think you would find that the words humility, submission, and sacrifice would be near the top of the list. To humble ourselves, to submit to another's authority, and to sacrifice what we want is not high on our "things to do" list. Frankly, we usually only do those things when we know we will somehow benefit.

In chapter 18, however, Jesus makes it clear that the keys to the Christian life hang on the ring of humility, submission, and sacrifice. So, as you read, consider how willing you are to live out those three things.

READ: LUKE 18

INVEST
In verses 1-5, what does the woman do?

Do you humble yourself daily to come into God's presence, recognizing that He alone can provide what you truly need, or do you try to work out most things by yourself?

What lesson does Jesus want us to learn from this poor widow?

In verses 10-14, who was filled with pride and who with humility? Which one did Jesus say was justified before God?

What do you think verse 17 means?

Children are used to submitting to, and relying on, an adult to provide for them. Is this how you are with God? Why or why not?

In the story of the rich young man (verses 18-30), what was this man unwilling to do?

How willing are you to sacrifice for the Lord?

In verses 31-33, how did Jesus state He would exemplify humility, submission, and sacrifice?

Are you willing to humble yourself and submit to God's will for your life regardless of what you may need to sacrifice? Why or why not?

PRAY
- Thank Jesus for exemplifying what it means to follow and serve God
- Confess, if necessary, not having much interest in being a humble, submissive, and sacrificing servant of God
- Ask the Lord to fill your life with humility
- Ask the Lord to mold you into a submissive and sacrificing servant

TRAINING
When it comes to humility, submission, and sacrifice, consider the following:
- Humility: Do you have to be first? Does it have to be done your way on your timetable? When others are leading things, are you constantly thinking about how you could do it better?
- Submission: Do you spend significant time in prayer before making a decision? Do you have a Christian mentor or accountability partner

who has permission to review your choices and decisions? Are you willing to wait for God's timing (which is often slower than our timing)?

- Sacrifice: If Jesus was waiting on your front porch right now and told you to give up everything and follow Him, what would you have trouble leaving behind? Do you sacrifice time to spend with God? Are you willing to sacrifice relationships that are hindering your walk with God? Are you ready to give up things in your life that are leading you into temptation or causing sin?

LUKE 19

START HERE

There are two sides to every coin. And, likewise, two sides to God—grace and truth. Some only choose to focus on the truth side of the coin, so when they present truths from the Bible, it's without any grace. That makes everything they say sound judgmental and condemning. Those people forget that there's no point in telling the truth if grace isn't around to offer the hope of a second chance.

Conversely, you also have those who focus solely on the grace side. But without truth, they become enablers to a life without clear boundaries. Those people forget that there's no reason to offer grace if truth doesn't exist to show us our need for a Savior.

Lastly, there are the ones who struggle and struggle to balance both truth and grace. For myself, I believe without a doubt that the Bible teaches both. The plain truth is that I am a sinner, and my sins are no better or worse than yours. But, here's the thing. When we experience the truth of our sinfulness colliding with the transforming power of God's grace, our eyes open to a whole new reality. A reality that we should want every single person in this world to understand, no matter who they are.

CONSIDER

Grace and truth. Love and Justice. We see both sides of God's character on display in chapter 19. Just as a bird has two wings and a coin has two sides, so the Lord's grace and love are balanced by His truth and justice. He forgives yet holds us accountable. He loves yet disciplines. He chastises yet embraces, and He angers yet never pushes us away.

As you read, consider if you have made God all about love or all about judgment instead of having a balanced view of the Lord.

READ: LUKE 19

INVEST

In verse 5, Jesus tells Zacchaeus, "I *must* be a guest in your home today." How do we see Jesus' desire to change lives in that comment?

Having experienced the grace and love of Jesus, how does Zacchaeus respond in verse 8?

How have you responded to Christ after experiencing His love and grace?

In the parable of the ten servants, how does the king reward those who responded well to his instructions?

How does he treat the one who did not respond well to his instructions?

How do we see both God's love and justice in this parable?

In verses 42-44, how do we see God's love and justice as well as His grace and truth?

Why is it important to realize that God loves you immeasurably but will exact consequences when necessary?

Do you have a balanced view of the Lord, or have you been guilty of seeing Him as all love or all judgment?

PRAY
- Thank God for being full of love and full of justice, full of grace and full of truth
- Confess, if necessary, having an unbalanced view of the Lord
- Ask the Lord to balance your view of Him and increase your understanding of His character
- Ask the Lord to grow, deepen, and mature you

TRAINING
Consider reading Randy Alcorn's short but excellent book, *The Grace and Truth Paradox: Responding with Christlike Balance*

LUKE 20

START HERE
What is the highest authority in the orange world?
The Pulp

An authoritative man walks into a bar…and orders everyone a round.

When it comes to authority, Oscar Wilde probably said it best, "Wherever there is a man who exercises authority; there is a man who resists authority."[53] Even when there is a God exercising authority, it seems there are still plenty willing to resist.

How about you?

CONSIDER
In the devotional from chapter 18, we spoke a great deal about humble submission. That is, the need to put aside pride and self so we can obediently follow the Lord's call on our lives. To do this, we must recognize Christ's authority over us. This recognition was something many in Jesus' day were not willing to make.

Today, as you read, consider if you are willing to submit humbly to that authority.

READ: LUKE 20

INVEST
Throughout chapter 20, Jesus' authority is challenged. In verses 9-19, for example, Jesus tells the story of tenant farmers who react in what way to their master's authority?

The first people that the farmers rejected were the master's servants. Today, we have the writings of God's servants collected in the Bible, and the first thing many reject in our day and age is the authority of those writings. Do you embrace the Bible as God's inerrant, holy Word?

Pride (wanting to be in total control) led to the tenant farmers rejecting even the master's own son. Does pride and the need for control cause you to reject Christ's work and guidance in your life?

In this chapter, we see multiple questions by the religious leaders. One sure sign of pride is the constant questioning of authority. When it comes to your relationship with the lord, do you find yourself questioning Him often? ("Is this Scripture really true?" "I don't like this verse. Do I need to obey it?" "The culture says this, so why do I have to follow that?" etc.)

If you are allowing your own thoughts or cultural trends to affect your view of God's truth, what must you do about this?

What does verse 46 say about the religious leaders?

Many who claim to be Christian today change their views and stances to find acceptance and praise within the culture. Why is this wrong?

What can you do to guard against such things?

PRAY
- Thank the Lord for His inerrant Word
- Confess, if necessary, questioning God's authority much too often
- Ask the Lord to deepen your understanding of His truth
- Ask the Lord to help you trust Him more and more each day

TRAINING
It is more important than ever to develop and maintain a strong Christian worldview. Take a few moments to look at the main components of worldview to see if you hold a biblical one.
- GOD—A secular worldview argues that there is no God, at least not as Christians would define Him. They might allow for an "entity" that exists in the cosmos, but this nebulous figure has no direct or personal role in our lives or world affairs. It is simply a "higher power" that

should have no bearing on our thoughts, our decisions, or how we live our lives. This, of course, is in direct opposition to what the Bible teaches. The Bible teaches that God is our Creator. He made the world, us, and everything else. Scripture further tells us of His revealing work, His incarnation to redeem a fallen people, and His imminent return to judge the world. Yes, God is active in our lives and intensely interested in His creation.

- MAN—Without a belief in an infinitely loving Creator God, you have little choice but to believe that we walk this earth today as the result of chance and evolution. In essence, you are just a random collection of atoms, molecules, and cells that happened together through blind chance over the course of millions, perhaps billions, of years. Conversely, a biblical worldview tells us that God formed man as the pinnacle of His creation. God created us in His image with the ability to love and to know as no other creature in the universe. We were created with these abilities because God wants us to love and know Him. He didn't create us out of a need for us. He created us out of an immeasurable desire to share His incredible love and fulfilling life with us. We were created as God's workmanship. We are wonderfully complex and loved creations made for a special purpose by an intensely personal God.

- TRUTH—When a society dismisses God and His purposeful creation of man from the equation, it is only a matter of time before truth falls as well. Without God, His Word, and His plan for mankind at the center, all objectivity is lost. Truth becomes relative and subjective. Soon we start to hear things like, "Well, that might be true for you, but it's not true for me." The values that we once held as basic and fundamental fall into a vague morass. Objective truth becomes situational, and few think twice about it. However, the Bible has over two hundred references to truth. Truth is real. Absolute truth is real. If you believe in Jesus, you must believe in truth. For Jesus said, *I am the way, the truth, and the life.* His truth is not based on situations, on human reasoning, on an era, or on cultural norms. His truth is based on Him and His Word.

- ETHICS—Once truth becomes relative, it is a short trip to ethics—which we'll define here as our view of "right vs. wrong"—becoming relative as well. If truth is no longer based on absolute, objective fact, then right and wrong will not be based on that either. The Bible, however, sees ethics from a completely different view. We cannot subjectively determine right and wrong. Rather, they are objectively judged by God. Lying was wrong in Moses' day, and it is wrong today.

Loving your enemy was right in Jesus' day, and it is right today. Right and wrong do not change with eras, cultures, elections, etc.

- KNOWLEDGE—A secular worldview will tell you that all knowledge is derived from human reasoning and scientific discovery. The Bible, however, declares that all knowledge flows from God and His revelation. This does not mean, despite the claims of many, that Christians are anti-reason or anti-science. It simply means that when all is said and done, our pursuit of knowledge starts with God, is guided by God, and ends with God.

LUKE 21

START HERE

When architect Sir Christopher Wren designed the interior of Windsor Town Hall near London in 1689, he built a ceiling supported by pillars. After city fathers had inspected the finished building, they decided the ceiling would not stay up and ordered Wren to put in some more pillars.

England's most celebrated architect didn't think the ceiling needed any more support, so he pulled a fast one. He added four pillars that did not do anything—they don't even reach the ceiling. The optical illusion fooled the municipal authorities, and today the four sham pillars amuse many a tourist.[54]

Sometimes our actions are very much like those four pillars. They are just for show to convince others of things that are not necessarily true about ourselves. Indeed, such actions might fool others, but never fool the Lord.

CONSIDER

We've talked a lot about pride over the last few chapters. The thing about pride is that it always focuses on the outside—"How do I look?" "How do others perceive me?" Pride usually doesn't do much focusing on the inward things that no one can see.

However, what matters most is not how we look or how people perceive us. The most important thing is whether or not God is pleased with the state of our heart, mind, and soul. As you read, consider if you focus more on how well people perceive you or how well God is pleased with you.

READ: LUKE 21

INVEST

In verses 1-4, we meet a woman, who, by appearance, seems stingy and cheap. Yet, what does Jesus say about her?

Some people may appear to be doing great things (like the rich giving large offerings), but the Lord knows the heart. He is only pleased with efforts (and offerings) that come from a desire to serve Him. With that in mind, how great is your desire to serve the Lord?

In verses 34-36, we read of Jesus urging us to keep our hearts from being dulled and distracted by the world. What tends to dull and distract you from Kingdom pursuits?

Verse 36 tells us to keep alert (be vigilant), so our hearts don't lose their passion for God. Where do you need to improve your vigilance?

What might need to be removed from, or lessened in, your life?

Between verses 1-4 and 34-36 is a long warning about the end times. One day Jesus will return. We need to ready for that day and help others be ready as well because once the Lord returns there will be no more second chances. So, what are you doing each day to stay ready?

What are you doing to help others get ready?

PRAY
- Thank the Lord for caring so deeply about your heart, mind, and soul
- Confess, if necessary, focusing more on your outside than your inside
- Ask the Lord to strengthen your heart, fill your soul, and instruct your mind
- Ask the Lord to show you where your heart might be dulled and distracted by the world

TRAINING
Guarding our hearts is one of our most pressing tasks. In fact, the Bible states that we should be doing this "above all else." Proverbs 4:23-27 states, *Above all else, guard your heart, for everything you do flows from it. Keep your mouth free of perversity; keep corrupt talk far from your lips. Let your eyes look straight ahead; fix your gaze directly before you. Give careful thought to the paths for your feet and be steadfast in all your ways. Do not turn to the right or the left; keep your foot from evil.*

- From this verse, we see the need to watch our words and our speech, staying away from angry words, foul language, blasphemy, rudeness, and more
- We must mind what we watch, being careful to avoid movies, TV shows, music, video games, internet sites that will damage our hearts and minds
- We should be careful where we go, removing ourselves from tempting situations that might cause us to sin
- We need to stay focused on the path God has for us, doing the things that will help us grow closer to Him—reading His Word, prayer, church, small groups, service projects, times of worship, etc.

LUKE 22

START HERE

The worst homing-pigeon: This historic bird was released in Pembrokeshire in June 1953 and was expected to reach its base that evening. It was returned by post, dead, in a cardboard box eleven years later from Brazil.

How about the least successful exhibition: The Royal Society for the Prevention of Accidents held an exhibition at Harrogate, Yorkshire. The entire display fell down.

And what about the least successful distribution of anti-virus software: A distinguished software development group at the Computer Studies Department of an Austrian University, proudly announced its most recent product and distributed it to selected testers. Unfortunately, a new type of virus infected the distribution disk which could not be detected or removed by the software. An awkward call back action was necessary.

Finally, the worst rugby match: In 1966 a rugby match between two teams from Wales was unexpectedly abandoned when it was discovered that neither team owned a ball.[55]

Failures indeed abound. And, sadly, many of those failures abound inside us. Thank goodness for a God who forgives!

CONSIDER

As you read through chapter 22, you will find betrayal, denial, and failure. Peter, Judas, and the rest of the disciples are the definition of a white hot mess. Now, it would be very easy to look in on this mess and shake our heads in disapproval. But how many times have we fallen into temptation and betrayed Christ in word, thought, and deed?

All too often.

As you read, don't shake your head at the disciples. No, instead, consider how much like them you may be.

READ: LUKE 22

INVEST
What happens with Judas in verses 3-4?

How often have you fallen into temptation and made a choice that betrayed the way of Christ?

What is happening in verses 55-62?

Imagine Peter connecting eyes with Jesus after denying Him three times. The Lord's gaze literally brought the big fisherman to bitter tears. Consider now that Christ can see, hear, and experience all our betrayals, denials, and failures yet still loves us more than words can express. What can you do to honor such amazing love?

Jesus provides the key to victory over temptation in verses 40 and 46? What is it?

How would pausing to pray every time you experience the pull of temptation change your life?

PRAY
- Thank the Lord for loving you beyond measure in spite of your many failures
- Confess, if necessary, not appreciating the depth of such love
- Ask the Lord to remind you to pray every time you experience temptation
- Ask the Lord to protect and guard your heart, mind, and soul

TRAINING
- Make a commitment to pray regularly
- Make a commitment to pause and pray each time you feel the tug of temptation

LUKE 23

START HERE

When my son, Kyle, was young, one of his favorite expressions was "a very lot."

"I like that a very lot."
"I want that a very lot."
"I do not like that a very lot."
"I want to go there a very lot."

Each time he would use this phrase, I would correct him. "Kyle, it's either 'a lot' or 'very much' not 'a very lot.'" However, he didn't seem to care for this grammatical correction a very lot, and I soon found myself saying it!

This is how life works. The more you spend time with someone, the more you begin to speak and act like that person. This is why we all need to be extra careful about who and what we spend time with.

CONSIDER

In chapter 23, we encounter several people who interact with Jesus on that fateful Good Friday. For this devotional, we will focus on five of them. Pilate, who seeks to please people over doing what is right. Barabbas, who becomes a literal example of Jesus dying in place of sinners. Simon, who must pick up the cross and follow Christ, the criminal who recognizes Christ as the Messiah, and Joseph of Arimathea, who refused to flow with his culture or the crowd.

As you read, consider how alike or dislike you are to these five people.

READ: LUKE 23

INVEST

What did Pilate do in verse 24? Why did he do this?

Do you tend to be negatively influenced by your peers or the culture? If so, what must you do about this?

How is Barabbas described in verse 25?

We are all no better than Barabbas, yet Christ (who had no sin) took our sin and died in our place. How can you honor that sacrifice today and every day?

What was Simon forced to do in verse 26?

Simon was the first person connected to Jesus who picked up the cross and followed. However, he was forced to do this. Today, Christ asks us to willingly deny ourselves, pick up our cross, and follow. How willing are you to live a life of sacrifice for Jesus?

How did one criminal recognize Christ for who He was in verse 42?

Do you live as though Christ is King of the Kingdom? Do you live to please your Lord and Savior?

What did Joseph do in verses 50-54?

How can you boldly stand for Christ and show all those around you that you are His follower?

PRAY
- Thank God for the examples He gives you in His Word
- Confess, if necessary, being more like Pilate than Joseph
- Ask the Lord to embolden you to stand for Him no matter what
- Ask the Lord to enable you to overcome the pull of the culture and the crowd

TRAINING
It is not an exact science to say that certain things will show whether or not someone is following Christ. As we discussed previously, we can do outward

acts, but that doesn't mean the inside has changed. However, below are a few things you can use to evaluate how well you are following Christ.

- Do you find your most profound sense of fulfillment and satisfaction in Christ?
- Do you influence the world around you for Jesus, or does the world influence you more?
- Does your walk match your talk? Do you live out what the Bible commands and the Lord requires?
- Do you have more peace than worry, more trust than doubt?
- Do you treat others the way you wish to be treated?
- Do you love people who irritate, annoy, and offend you?
- When things don't go your way, do you maintain your faith and your trust?
- Jesus says, "If you love Me, you will obey Me." Do you obey Christ out of a desire to honor Him?

LUKE 24

START HERE

While I was in seminary, the church I attended had a Christmas tradition. The tradition was simple. A Christmas tree would be erected, and everyone was encouraged to bring in an ornament that was special to them. Then, on a Sunday morning in December, those willing brought their ornament to the tree, faced the congregation, and explained why they choose that particular ornament.

Since I was teaching Sunday School at this church, everyone assumed that I would be bringing an ornament and participating in this tradition. There was just one small problem. My seminary sat 1100 miles from home, and I had no "special" Christmas ornaments with me.

Now, I could have gone out and bought an ornament. But if you look up seminary student in the dictionary, it would say, "See: POOR." I didn't have the money to buy an ornament. And, even if I did, what would I say? "This ornament is special to me because it was on clearance at Wal-Mart."

As the time for the tree decorating service drew near, I was getting desperate. Rummaging through the dorm, I came across a closet that contained a box of leftover Christmas stuff. Inside were broken ceramic pieces, ripped strands of garland, malfunctioning holiday lights, and, yes, one lone, (and free) ornament. Better yet, not only was it free, it was red. I immediately thought I could say something about Jesus coming that first Christmas so He could one day spill His blood for our sins. This was getting good!

Excitedly, I pulled the bulb from the box only to discover why it had been left there in the first place. It was broken. The metal crown that clasped around the top of the bulb was missing as well as its hanger. Moreover, on closer inspection, the bulb's paint was dirty and smudged. My initial excitement ebbed quickly.

Scrounging through the box, I found the metal crown and brought it and the bulb back to my dorm room. There, I started working to put it all back together. I took a paperclip and shaped it into a hanger and fixed it to the crown. After that, I carefully glued the crown back onto the bulb. Once dry, I set out to polish, clean, and buff that little bulb, trying to get it back to the way it was designed and created to look.

During that process, a realization struck me. This is what God does with us. God finds us broken and stained. Seeing us in this condition, He begins working on us, seeking to heal us, to put us back together, and to restore us to our original design and created purpose.

Truly, while restoring that little broken bulb, God provided me the reason it was special. We are broken, but God wants to make us whole. We are stained, but God wants to cleanse us. This is why Jesus came. He came so that our brokenness could be mended, our wounds could be healed, our sins could be forgiven, our original image restored, and our created purpose realized.

CONSIDER

An empty tomb means forgiveness, redemption, and new life are possible for us all. In chapter 22, Peter denies the Lord three times, then flees into the night. In chapter 23, while Jesus suffers and dies an agonizing death, the big fisherman is nowhere to be found…but then chapter 24.

News reaches Peter that Jesus' tomb is empty. He rushes out to see and finds the story true. "Could He be alive?" the denying disciple must be wondering. "And could He ever forgive me?"

Verse 34 gives the answer. "The Lord has really risen! He appeared to Peter."

Jesus tracked down Peter to offer forgiveness and a new beginning. Today, the Lord continues to do the same. As you read, consider where you might need to embrace Jesus' fresh offer of forgiveness and a new beginning.

READ: LUKE 24

INVEST

In verse 12, what did Peter do when he heard the women's story?

Before that time, Peter must have been feeling much like the two men walking to Emmaus. How do we find them in verse 17?

Have there been times in your life when you've felt helpless or hopeless?

How can the news of chapter 24 encourage you during those times?

When you fall short, sin, or struggle, how can the story of Jesus tracking down Peter reassure you?

What is our job according to verse 47?

With whom are you currently sharing the Good News?

Who else might you add to that list?

PRAY
- Thank Jesus for the message of the empty tomb
- Confess, if necessary, running from Christ instead of running to Him when you sin
- Ask the Lord to provide you with opportunities to share the Good News
- Ask the Lord to encourage your faith

TRAINING
- Don't let the devil whisper in your ear that you are not forgiven
- Embrace Christ's resurrection which gives you new life
- When the devil lies to you, recall the cross

JOHN 1

START HERE

"While the other three gospels portray Jesus as the King, the Servant, and the Son of Man, John portrays Jesus as the Son of God. John stated his theme more clearly than any of the other gospel writers. He wrote so that his readers might 'believe that Jesus is the Christ, the Son of God,' so that they may have life in His name (John 20:31)."[56]

"Jesus' identity as the Son of God sets Him apart from any other man who ever lived. He carries with Him the transcendence that comes only with God Himself. Therefore, His work on our behalf makes our salvation sure. Because He is God, His sacrifice on the cross has eternal implications, unlike the limited effect of the animal sacrifices in the Old Testament…For readers of John's gospel, the question is a simple, though significant, one: Do you believe that Jesus is Lord? If you believe, you will receive eternal life, claiming the truth that you will one day live in the presence of God in a place with no more pain, no more tears, and no more death."[57]

CONSIDER

The Gospel of John is much different than the other Gospels. Matthew, Mark, and Luke are known as the Synoptic Gospels because they each give a general synopsis, or relatively chronological biography, of Jesus' life. John, however, does not do this.

This Gospel does not have extended times of teaching like Matthew. (There are only two.) It does not focus on the many miracles that Jesus performed like Mark. (There are only seven mentioned.) And it does not add extra story details as the book of Luke so often does. Instead, John centers on the person of Jesus—the Savior of the world, fully man and fully God.

Entering chapter 1, you will not find John starting with a birth narrative. No, he jumps right into explaining Jesus' divine nature. As you read, consider how Jesus—God in the Flesh—has impacted your life.

READ: JOHN 1

INVEST

How does John explain who Jesus is in verses 1-5 and 14-15?

Throughout the Gospel of John, one of the central metaphors for Jesus is that He is "the Light." How do we see this in verses 5-9?

How has Jesus shined a light in your life?

What is the Good News of verse 12?

In verses 35-46, we see the Gospel spread as friends and relatives seek to bring people to Jesus. (Andrew gets Peter; Philip finds Nathanael, etc.) Who can you bring to Jesus by sharing the Good News with them?

When will you share with the people you just listed?

PRAY
- Thank Jesus for being the Son of God and the Light of the World
- Confess, if necessary, not allowing His light to shine through you
- Ask the Lord to let your light shine brightly
- Ask the Lord to use you to spread the Gospel

TRAINING
- Keep praying for the five people you have on your prayer card
- Seek opportunities to share with at least one of them this week
- As we've discussed before, adopt a country to pray for and/or add actors, directors, singers, politicians, and others in public/influential positions to your prayer list

JOHN 2

START HERE

Up until the age of ten, it was not uncommon for my son to have a pair of red cheeks. No, it wasn't because he was out playing in the cold, because I am not talking about his face. I'm talking about another set of cheeks!

However, when he turned ten, we went on a "man weekend" and discussed how turning double digits was a big deal—one that required a new level of maturity from him and also a new way to be disciplined when that maturity was lacking. Instead of spanks and time in his room staring at the ceiling, there would be "loss of privileges." Video game and TV time, snacks and soda, hanging out with friends, some or all of those things evaporated if his behavior needed "modifying."

Of course, after this went into effect, it was not uncommon for Kyle to literally beg for a spanking and an extended time-out over losing video games for three days. Yes, growing up can be hard!

Nevertheless, regardless of the consequence, afterward I would sit down with him, put my arm around his shoulder, and let him know that he was loved. It was now time to start fresh with a clean slate. During these times, it was my hope that Kyle would come to understand the grace and truth (love and justice) of God. With the Lord, consequences always come to those who deserve them, but grace always offers a fresh start and a second chance.

CONSIDER

In John 2, we experience two events in the ministry of Jesus—one of His first and one of His last. As we noted yesterday, the Gospel of John is unlike the other Gospels in that it does not concern itself with timelines. Rather, it seeks to show us exactly who Jesus is—His character, His attributes, His humanity, and His deity.

Chapter 2 first shows us His mercy and grace at the wedding of Cana, then it shifts to His truth and justice seen in the clearing of the Temple (an event that Matthew, Mark, and Luke put near the end of Jesus' earthly ministry). By contrasting these two attributes of Jesus at the beginning of his book, John shows us that Jesus is someone filled with grace for those who need it, but also someone ready to exact justice on those who need a swift kick in the hindquarters!

As you read, consider how both Jesus' grace and His truth have worked in your life.

READ: JOHN 2

INVEST

How do we see the grace and provision of Jesus in verses 1-10?

To run out of drink at a wedding ceremony (which usually lasted up to a week in Jewish culture) would have been the height of embarrassment for the host and his family, marring the joyous occasion. It was truly a great gesture by Jesus to spare such embarrassment. How have you experienced God's grace sparing you from heartache, stress, embarrassment, or more?

How do we see Jesus' truth and justice in verses 13-17?

The religious leaders (in verses 18-20) refused to accept Jesus' rebuke. Do you accept, and grow from, the consequences the Lord brings into your life?

Some focus solely on God's grace and treat Him as a doting "Grandpa in the Sky." Others focus on God's justice and view Him as a harsh, abusive Father. Why are both characterizations wrong?

Why is it important to realize that the Trinity reaches out with grace when we are in need, but also disciplines us when we are living in disobedience?

PRAY
- Thank God for His grace and His truth
- Confess, if necessary, having a lopsided view of God
- Ask the Lord to show you His grace where you are in need
- Ask the Lord to correct you when necessary

TRAINING

Consider reading two short articles that explain God's love and justice:

- Go to gotquestions.org and type in "What does it mean that God is just?"
- Go to gotquestions.org and type in "What does it mean that God is love?"

JOHN 3

START HERE

Some years ago, on a hot summer day in south Florida, a little boy decided to go for a swim in the old swimming hole behind his house. In a hurry to dive into the cool water, he ran out the back door, leaving behind shoes, socks, and shirt as he went.

He flew into the water, not realizing that as he swam toward the middle of the lake, an alligator was swimming toward the shore.

His father, working in the yard, saw the two moving toward each other. In utter fear, he ran toward the water, yelling to his son as loudly as he could.

Hearing his voice, the little boy became alarmed and made a U-turn to swim to his father. It was too late. Just as he reached his father, the alligator reached him. From the dock, the father grabbed his little boy by the arms as the alligator snatched his legs. An incredible tug-of-war between the two began. The alligator was much stronger than the father, but the father was much too passionate to let go. A farmer happened to drive by, heard his screams, raced from his truck, took aim and shot the alligator.

Remarkably, after weeks and weeks in the hospital, the little boy survived. The vicious attack left his legs extremely scarred while deep scratches, where his father's fingernails dug into his flesh, covered his arms.

The newspaper reporter interviewing the boy after the trauma asked if he would show him his scars. The boy lifted his pant legs. And then, with obvious pride, he said to the reporter, "But look at my arms. I have great scars on my arms, too. I have them because my dad wouldn't let go."

You and I can identify with that little boy. We have scars, too. No, not from an alligator, but the scars of a painful past. Some of those scars are unsightly and have caused us deep regret. But, some wounds, are because God has refused to let go. In the midst of your struggle, He's been there holding on to you.[58]

CONSIDER

If you were ever uncertain as to why Jesus took on flesh and entered into humanity, all you have to do is read John 3. In this chapter, we clearly see

God's love and Christ's compassion, and the lengths they will travel never to let us go.

As you read, consider how you have responded to this love and compassion. Is the response humble surrender or stubborn refusal?

READ: JOHN 3

INVEST

In verses 1-8, Nicodemus wants to know how to experience the Kingdom of God. How does Jesus respond?

Nicodemus seems mostly clueless about what it means to be born again. In this respect, our friend Nic is like many of the people all around us. To them, how would you explain what being born again means?

In Numbers 21, God punishes the Hebrews for sin and stubbornness by sending poisonous snakes. The only cure was to look up at a bronze snake that Moses affixed to a pole. How does Jesus allude to something similar that would be used by Him to cure us of the poison of sin (verses 14-15)?

What does John 3:16 state?

We spoke in the previous devotional about God's grace and justice. How do we see this again in verses 18-21?

What does John 3:30 say?

Are Jesus and His will becoming more and more while you and your will are becoming less and less? Why or why not?

In verse 36, how do we see that belief must be coupled with obedience?

We know from James 2 that many say they believe in God, but then so do demons! Demons, however, do not obey. The key to true belief is to follow through on that belief. How are you doing with that?

PRAY

- Thank God for so loving the world that He gave His one and only Son
- Confess, if necessary, thinking you can believe in God without obeying Him
- Ask the Lord to give you an obedient heart
- Ask the Lord to help you become less and less so that He can become more and more

TRAINING

Is Jesus becoming more and more in your life? Consider a few things:

- Do you earnestly seek His will before making decisions?
- Do you guard your heart and mind against inappropriate words and images that often fill movies, music, TV shows, video games, the internet, and more?
- Does God win all scheduling conflicts in your life?
- Are you daily studying Scripture?
- Do you regularly attend church and a small group?
- Do you pray multiple times a day, including at least one extended time of prayer?

JOHN 4

START HERE
Growing up, I thought that my father had a superpower. He could tell my mom was upset just by how she was sitting. I would look at her and not think a thing was wrong, but my dad seemed to know something was up telepathically.

Now, married myself, I have developed this same superpower…all without getting bit by a radioactive spider, falling into a vat of nuclear goo, or being exposed to gamma rays. To the world, my wife can appear carefree. But, by certain mannerisms, I know something is up (and I quickly need to figure out what I did wrong!)

As I am sure you know (especially if you are married), this isn't really a superpower. It is something that develops as you get to know someone. The more time you spend someone, the more you understand that person.

The same is true in our relationship with the Lord.

CONSIDER
In chapter 4, a simple woman is simply trying to get water from a well. In the process of doing so, she encounters Christ. As her time with him increases, so does her understanding of who He is and what He has come to accomplish.

As you read, consider if (by the sheer amount of time you have spent with the Lord) you are starting to understand Him more and more.

READ: JOHN 4

INVEST
Chart the progression of how the people in the story address Jesus in verses 9, 11, 15, 19 (2 things), 28, and 42:

As Jesus spends time with the woman, and with the Samaritan village, He goes from "you" to "sir" to "prophet" to "maybe the Messiah" to "indeed the Savior of the world." What does this show you?

How much time do you spend with Jesus each day?

Do you think this time is sufficient to fully get to know and understand Him? Why or why not?

Realize that the woman went to the well at noon because it was the hottest part of the day, and she thought no one would be there at that time. She did not want to get the stares from people because of her lifestyle. But then, after experiencing Christ, she is standing in the center of town talking to everyone! With that in mind, would you say that time with Jesus has changed you in significant ways?

If not, what might this tell you about the amount of time you are spending with Christ?

PRAY
- Thank Jesus for His power to transform your life
- Confess, if necessary, not spending enough time with the Lord
- Ask the Lord to make you more and more like Him
- Ask the Lord to fill you with a desire to spend time with Him

TRAINING
It seems effortless for us to spend an hour watching a gripping drama on TV, to play two hours of video games, to surf the web for an entire evening, etc. Yet, when it comes to spending thirty minutes with the Lord, we wonder how we will find the time! With that in mind:
- Think through your daily schedule
- How much TV do you watch each day? How much time is spent with video games, the internet, phone apps, reading fiction novels, perusing magazines, hobbies, sports, etc.?
- What can you cut out of (or shorten in) your schedule to deepen your time with the Lord?

JOHN 5

START HERE

An Amish boy and his father were visiting a mall. They were amazed by almost everything they saw, but especially by two shiny, silver walls that could move apart and back together again. The boy asked his father, "What is this, Father?"

Dad responded, "Son, I have never seen such a thing in my life."

While the boy and his father were still studying this amazing contraption, an elderly woman in a wheelchair rolled up to the moving walls and pressed a button. The walls opened, and the lady rolled between them into a small room. The walls closed behind her, while the boy and his father watched on.

About a minute later, the silver walls parted again and out stepped a beautiful young woman.

Amazed, the father turned to his son, "Hurry! Go get your mother."[59]

All of us should long to be transformed and to see transformation happen in the lives of all those around us. Thankfully, through Christ, that transformation can happen without the need for an elevator!

CONSIDER

As we know, Jesus came to offer forgiveness of sins and salvation to the world. Everything He said and did was designed to fulfill those purposes. For example, in chapter 5, Jesus miraculously heals a man who battled sickness for thirty-eight long years. A tremendous act of God, but not Jesus' primary focus. Christ didn't heal that man so he could be physically well. Jesus healed that man so he could be spiritually well.

Using the miracle, Jesus launches into a teaching time where He explains that He came to be a light in the dark, a healer to the sick, and a life-giver to those who are spiritually dead. As you read, consider that Jesus is much more interested in transforming your heart and mind than healing your body.

READ: JOHN 5

INVEST

After healing the man, what does Jesus tell him in verse 14?

Jesus bluntly shares this truth because He understands that being sick isn't nearly as bad as being unforgiven. Without salvation and new life, being healthy doesn't mean much. How about you? With which are you more concerned? Your physical health or your spiritual health?

Why is your spiritual health much more important than your physical health?

What does Jesus say about salvation in verses 24, 26, 29, and 39-40?

How is your spiritual life right now? Where might you need Jesus' touch?

How about those around you? Who needs a spiritual touch from Jesus?

It is not uncommon for churches and small groups to take prayer requests. During these times, it seems eighty percent or more of the requests deal with physical issues while only a small percentage deal with spiritual issues. What can you do to help flip that in your church or small group?

PRAY
- Thank Jesus for opening a way to salvation
- Confess, if necessary, a greater focus on physical needs over spiritual needs
- Ask the Lord to work in your areas of spiritual need
- Ask the Lord to work spiritually in the lives of those around you

TRAINING

Consider the following ways to pray for spiritual needs:
- Pray for unity in the body of Christ in general and in your church specifically

- Pray for God's people to be open to the will and guiding hand of the Spirit
- Pray for hearts to be open to the truth of the Gospel
- Pray to be led from temptation and delivered from the evil one
- Pray for spiritual maturity and growth
- Pray for pastors, missionaries, Sunday School teachers, children and youth leaders, and others in Christian ministry

JOHN 6

START HERE

The average three year-old thinks like this: If it's mine, it's mine. If it's yours, it's mine. If I like it, it's mine. If I can take it from you, it's mine. If it looks like mine, it's mine. If I think it's mine, it's mine. If I saw it first, it's mine. If I had it then put it down, it's still mine. If you had it then put it down, it's now mine. If it's broken, it's yours.

Yes, that does sound like the average three year-old. But, sadly, it also sounds like many adults I know! As Dave Barry once said, "You can only be young once, but you can be immature forever."

CONSIDER

In Natalie Grant's magnificent song, "More than Anything, " she sings:
Help me want the Healer
More than the healing
Help me want the Savior
More than the saving
Help me want the Giver
More than the giving
Oh, help me want You, Jesus
More than anything

Those are great lyrics, ones that we should all strive to live out. Unfortunately, in our Scripture for today, many who have been following Christ seem to want the healing more than the Healer, the saving more than the Savior, and the giving more than the Giver.

As you read, consider why you follow Christ.

READ: JOHN 6

INVEST

According to verse 2, why are the people following Jesus?

What does Jesus say to them in verse 26?

In verse 29, what does Jesus state God wants the people to do?

As we have discussed already, the Greek word often translated *believe* in the New Testament carries with it the idea of a pledge to live out what you say you believe. With that in mind, we can read verse 29 as Jesus saying, "The only work God wants from you is for you to faithfully live out your belief in Me regardless of what you get or don't get." Is this how you view life in Christ? Why or why not?

How do the people respond to Jesus in verse 66?

How do you respond when God doesn't do things the way you would like?

What does Peter say to Jesus in verses 68-69?

Are you clinging to Christ no matter what?

PRAY
- Thank Jesus for being Healer, Savior, and Giver
- Confess, if necessary, wanting things from God more than you want God Himself
- Ask the Lord to help you live out your belief in Him
- Ask the Lord to strengthen your commitment and resolve

TRAINING
The Greek word used for *belief* in the New Testament can be thought of like a marriage pledge, where one promises to stay committed for better, for worse, for richer, for poorer, in sickness and in health. With that in mind, consider if you have that level of commitment with the Lord.

JOHN 7

START HERE

A few years back, the hose on my vacuum cleaner developed a tear. I thought it would be very simple to replace the hose, so I went online and ordered a new one. When it arrived, I figured it would take me five minutes to switch out the hoses. Wow! I was wrong!

To remove the original hose, I had to remove the hose casing. Once the casing was off, I discovered yet another piece needed removal, then another, and still another! Soon, I had vacuum parts scattered around my living room, and I was about to lose my sanctification!

Things are usually not as simple as they seem. When you take the time to get below the surface, you often find there's a whole lot more going on. Of course, this is not only true with vacuums. It is true with all manner of things, especially with relationships.

CONSIDER

In our reading for today, Jesus declares, *"Look beneath the surface, so you can judge correctly."* Unfortunately, this kind of "looking" doesn't happen as often as it should. Many times, we hear a bit of gossip or a hint of rumor and instantly pass judgment. Indeed, it's a miracle that we all haven't sprained something, as we jump to from one conclusion to another with just minimal information.

Worse, we let such things creep into our relationship with the Lord. When something terrible happens, we assume God is mad at us or no longer loves us. Conversely, when something breaks our way, we're convinced God is very pleased with how we are doing.

Rarely, in our relationship with God or others, do we dig deeper. As you read, consider how far beneath the surface you are willing to go in your relationships.

READ: JOHN 7

INVEST

Instead of searching the Scriptures intently, or having an in-depth conversation with Jesus to determine if He really is the Messiah, what do Jesus' relatives do in verses 1-5?

What do we read about the crowd in verses 12, 25-27, and 40-44?

What do we read about the Pharisees and the religious leaders in verses 32-36 and 47-49?

There is much confusion and divided opinion about Jesus, but not much diligent searching for truth. (For example, it wouldn't have taken much to discover verse 42 was true of Jesus.) One of the few to defend Jesus is Nicodemus who went deeper with Christ in chapter 3. What does he say in verse 50?

It took courage for Nicodemus to go against his peers and his culture. But after meeting with Jesus in chapter 3, the old Pharisee was convinced that Jesus was who He said He was. Are you taking the time—in prayer, Bible study, church attendance, and other growth opportunities—to get below the surface with Jesus?

What more could you be doing?

PRAY
- Thank Jesus for all that He is
- Confess, if necessary, not going beneath the surface as often as you should in your relationship with Christ and others
- Ask the Lord to take you deeper in Him
- Ask the Lord to help you dig deeper in your relationship with friends, family, coworkers, neighbors, classmates, etc.

TRAINING
- It may be uncomfortable—perhaps even painful—but start digging

down to the root of issues inside yourself

- Dig deeper in your relationship with others. Are you having struggles with a particular person? Dedicate yourself to figuring out exactly why
- Go deep in your relationship with Christ. Invest the time and energy needed to grow and mature in Him
- When you hear gossip, don't just assume it to be true or accurate. Take time to get the facts. (Or, better, stay away from gossip altogether!)

JOHN 8

START HERE

The Bible says that all of us have sinned. This means we are all guilty. You think that is bad news? Oh, we're just getting started, for the Bible also declares that there is a penalty for all of this sin. Death! So, now, not only are we guilty, but we are on death row. Talk about bringing a skunk to a garden party!

Yet, wonder of wonders, the Bible further tells of a God who would take on flesh, enter humanity, and die in the place of those who rejected Him. What great news! The death sentence need not apply. We can step out of prison. We can be free.

I don't know where you are in your walk with the Lord. Perhaps you have yet to walk out of the prison cell. Sure, you know Jesus, but you still feel trapped by lies, greed, anger, resentment, lust, immorality, gossip, etc. You have not stepped into the freedom that is yours.

Perhaps you've been struggling with the same issue year after year after year. Maybe it's your marriage or a struggle with a certain sin that keeps beating you. Regardless of what it is, you are at the point of hopelessness. All your brain will tell you is, "It's been this long, and it's just going to continue. It will be yet another day, another week, another month, another year. This will never end."

Don't believe it! Jesus has come with pardon papers in hand. He has come to set you free, and when the Son sets you free, you are free indeed. He has the power to heal your marriage, to defeat any issue, and to overcome that sin. Don't give up. Freedom and hope are here in the person of Jesus Christ.

CONSIDER

John 8:32 is one of the most famous, and most misused, verses in all of the Bible—*"You will know the truth, and the truth will set you free."* It is not uncommon for even non-Christians to quote the last part of this Scripture as if to say, "If you tell the truth, you won't feel guilty about lying anymore." However, that is *not* the point Jesus was trying to make at all.

In context, Jesus states, *"You are truly my disciples if you remain faithful to my teachings. And you will know the truth, and the truth will set you free."*

What Christ is actually saying here is, "The more you draw close to Me in obedience, the more you will understand that I am Truth, and it is I alone that can set you free from sin, shame, and guilt."

As you read, carefully consider the words of Jesus that you might understand fully.

READ: JOHN 8

INVEST

How do we see Jesus setting someone free from sin, shame, and guilt in verses 1-11?

Just "encountering" Jesus is not enough for life change. How does the Lord make this plain in verse 11?

How do the Pharisees misunderstand Jesus in verses 13-20?

How do the "regular folk" misunderstand Jesus in verses 22-27?

In verse 36, how does Jesus clarify who the Truth is and who really sets someone free?

Have you any experience with people misunderstanding the Scriptures or who Jesus is?

Has this ever been a problem in your own life? If yes, how so?

What can be done to ensure that you truly understand who Jesus is and why He came to earth?

In what ways can you share this message with others?

PRAY
- Thank Jesus for being the way, the truth, and the life
- Confess, if necessary, misusing Scripture or misunderstanding who Jesus is
- Ask the Lord to deepen your relationship with the Son, so that you can live in freedom
- Ask the Lord to provide you with opportunities to share the Truth with others

TRAINING

Consider three simple steps to deepening your own walk with Christ while simultaneously helping others begin a walk with Christ:
- Step 1 – Listen – Spend time investing in the Scriptures, devotions, and Bible study. Learn and grow as you experience the Word of God
- Step 2 – Follow – James 1:22-25 reads, *But don't just listen to God's word. You must do what it says. Otherwise, you are only fooling yourselves. For if you listen to the word and don't obey, it is like glancing at your face in a mirror. You see yourself, walk away, and forget what you look like. But if you look carefully into the perfect law that sets you free, and if you do what it says and don't forget what you heard, then God will bless you for doing it.* It isn't enough to just study the Bible; we need to live it out in our words, actions, and attitudes
- Step 3 – Share – As we deepen in our relationship with the Lord, and begin to emulate Him more and more, we should naturally be offering Him to the world, looking for opportunities to share the Good News and grow the Kingdom

JOHN 9

START HERE

At the age of seventeen, Joni Eareckson dove head first into a lake without realizing how shallow the water was. Breaking her neck, she became paralyzed from the shoulders down. After two years of rehabilitation, she emerged with new skills and a fresh determination to help others in similar situations.

During her rehabilitation, Joni spent long months learning how to paint with a brush between her teeth. Her high-detail art paintings and prints are sought after and collected. Her best-selling autobiography *Joni* and the feature film of the same name have been translated into many languages, introducing her to people around the world.

She has gone on to write over fifty books, become a regular columnist for several magazines, be inducted into the Christian Booksellers' Association's Hall of Honor, and receive the Gold Medallion Lifetime Achievement Award from the Evangelical Christian Publishers Association.

In 2002, Joni received the William Ward Ayer Award for excellence from the National Religious Broadcasters' Association. In 2012, the National Religious Broadcasters Association inducted her into its Hall of Fame. In 2015, Moody Radio awarded Joni its prestigious Robert Neff Award for distinguished spiritual excellence in religious broadcasting. And in 2017, Biola University conferred upon Joni its highly acclaimed Charles W. Colson Courage & Conviction Award.[60]

Some pout over their shortcomings and limitations. Others rise above and allow God to use those same shortcomings and limitations for His glory and the benefit of others. Which do you do?

CONSIDER

In Bible times, the Jews believed anyone born with a physical or mental defect was the result of sinful parents under God's punishment. In chapter 9, however, Jesus is going to make it clear that anything we go through in life, no matter how hard or difficult, is an opportunity to glorify God. We can put the Lord's power on display as we trust in Him to carry us through whatever situation or struggle we find ourselves in.

As you read, consider if you view adverse events as punishment from God or as opportunities to glorify Him.

READ: JOHN 9

INVEST

How do we see the disciples misunderstanding why bad things happen in verses 1-2?

How does Jesus clarify things in verses 3-6?

How do we see the blind man's life change throughout chapter 9 as he slowly comes to recognize who is working in his life?

Just as in John 4, we can see, by the way Jesus is addressed, a deepening in understanding. Chart the progression in verses 11, 17, 25, 33, and 38:

Through the difficulty of his blindness, followed by persecution, the man at the center of the narrative goes from calling Jesus "man" (verse 11) to calling Him "Lord" (verse 38). Does your trust in Jesus increase or decrease during difficult times?

If you answered "decrease," what lessons can you take from this chapter?

PRAY
- Thank God for the opportunities He provides you to glorify Him with your life
- Confess, if necessary, viewing your difficulties through the wrong lens
- Ask the Lord to use you to glorify Him even when things are difficult
- Ask the Lord to do awesome things in and through your life

TRAINING

Understanding why God allows us to go through difficulties is the first step to being able to glorify Him come what may, so consider the following:

- Difficult times test our faith, showing us where we are weak and where we are strong
- Difficult times test our obedience. Anyone can obey when life is easy, but what about when life most definitely isn't easy?
- Difficult times cause us to rely on God. Again, when life is sunshine and butterflies, do you find yourself clinging to the Lord? It is during the trying times that we seek to draw near to His presence
- Difficult times often reveal our purpose. Sometimes the greatest tragedies or struggles in our lives can become our greatest avenue of service to the Lord. Losing a child leads you to become a grief counselor. Overcoming a porn addiction directs you to lead a Celebrate Recovery group, etc.

JOHN 10

START HERE

One day, a police officer on patrol noticed a man driving with a sheep in the front seat. Pulling that car over, the officer asked, "What are you doing with a sheep in the passenger seat!?!"

"I'm taking it to the zoo," came a quick reply. Finding that answer acceptable, the policeman let the driver go.

However, the following week, the same patrolman again noticed the same man driving with a sheep in the passenger seat. Once more the officer pulled the car over. "I thought you told me that you were taking that sheep to the zoo!"

"I did," the man answered. "We had such a great time that we're going to the beach this weekend!"[61]

Why the sheep joke, you ask? Keep reading.

CONSIDER

Sheep don't have a whole lot going for them. Our fluffy friends have no true defense mechanisms—no venom, no claws, no fangs, no speed, no muscle, no stink spray, no nothing. And on top of all that nothing, sheep actually bare their necks when attacked! These woeful wool makers have only one real chance at avoiding a baaaad end—stay close to the shepherd. To live, a sheep must bond to the voice of its shepherd and always stay within earshot.

We are no different. We must bond to the voice of our Good Shepherd and follow Him wherever He leads, always making sure to stay within earshot. Otherwise, we will find ourselves as easy prey to that roaring lion that prowls around looking for victims to devour (1 Peter 5:8).

As you read, consider how well ewe are following the Shepherd of your soul each day.

READ: JOHN 10

INVEST
What is the devil's purpose according to verse 10?

What is the Good Shepherd's purpose according to verse 10?

What do verses 3, 4, 14, 16, and 27 have in common?

A sheep's brain will imprint on its shepherd's voice as the shepherd speaks to it. When successfully imprinted, thirty people can call for a sheep, but it will only follow one. How about you? Do you know your Shepherd's voice well, or are you easily led astray by other voices?

What can help you better learn the Shepherd's voice?

How often do you pray, study Scripture, talk about faith matters with others, listen to worship music, etc.?

Who is instructing you in the ways of the Shepherd?

Who are you instructing?

PRAY
- Thank Jesus for being the Good Shepherd who lays down His life for the sheep
- Confess, if necessary, being led astray by voices within our culture
- Ask the Lord to help you recognize your Shepherd's voice
- Ask the Lord to use you to help others recognize His voice

TRAINING
Have you ever been in a crowded place where the buzz of dozens of conversations is almost deafening? Yet, even in a place like that, when your spouse or your child calls out, you instantly recognize the voice. Why? You

know your family so well that you can pick out their voices almost anywhere.

As Christians, we should all be like that with Jesus. Here are some things that can help us better hear and recognize our Shepherd's voice:

- Daily Bible study
- Weekly small group studies
- Weekly Sunday school classes
- Weekly worship services
- Constant prayer—where you listen more than you talk

JOHN 11

START HERE

There was a woman who had been diagnosed with a terminal illness and given just three months to live. As she was getting her affairs in order, she contacted her pastor and had him come to her house to discuss certain aspects of her final wishes.

Over the course of a couple hours, they discussed which songs to be sung at the service, what Scriptures to be read, and what outfit she wanted to be buried in. All seemed to be in order when the woman made one more request. "There's one more thing, Pastor."

"What's that?" came the pastor's reply.

"This is very important," the woman continued. "I want to be buried with a fork in my right hand." The pastor stood looking at the woman, not knowing quite what to say. "That surprises you, doesn't it?"

"Well, to be honest, I'm puzzled by the request," said the pastor.

The woman explained. "In all my years of attending church socials and potluck dinners, I always remember that when the dishes of the main course were being cleared, someone would inevitably lean over and say, 'Keep your fork.' It was my favorite part because I knew that something better was coming like velvety chocolate cake or deep-dish apple pie. So, I just want people to see me there in that casket with a fork in my hand, and I want them to wonder "What's with the fork?'. Then I want you to tell them: 'She wants everyone to know to keep their fork—for the best is yet to come.'"[62]

CONSIDER

In John 11:25, the Bible says, *Jesus told her, "I am the resurrection and the life. Anyone who believes in me will live, even after dying. Everyone who lives in me and believes in me will never die. Do you believe this…?"*

Death has a one hundred percent success rate. It will come to us all, but that doesn't mean it has to win. Because of Jesus, death can be the loser!

1 Corinthians 15:54-57 wonderfully declares, *"Death is swallowed up in victory. O death, where is your victory? O death, where is your sting?" For*

sin is the sting that results in death, and the law gives sin its power. But thank God! He gives us victory over sin and death through our Lord Jesus Christ.

As you read, consider if you are living in that victory through Jesus Christ!

READ: JOHN 11

INVEST
According to Jesus in verse 4, what was the point of Lazarus's sickness and eventual death?

In John 9, we discussed how God is often most glorified as we live out our faith during the worst of times. How can living out your faith when dealing with the loss of a loved one also bring great glory to God?

What did Jesus do for Lazarus?

What Jesus did for Lazarus, He will do for all those who die trusting in His name. How can that give you hope even during the most difficult of times?

In verse 50, how did Caiaphas unwittingly prophecy about what Jesus would do?

Jesus suffered a seeming defeat in His death on the cross, yet that death brought victory to the billions who have trusted in His name. How can such knowledge encourage you when it is your time to pass through death's door?

How can you use this knowledge to encourage others?

PRAY
- Thank Jesus for giving us victory over sin and death
- Confess, if necessary, fearing death

- Ask the Lord to fill you with the hope of knowing that He has prepared an eternal home for you
- Ask the Lord to use you in the lives of others who are undergoing loss or hardship

TRAINING
- Consider reading the book *A Grief Observed,* written by C.S. Lewis after dealing with the tragic loss of his wife, Joy

JOHN 12

START HERE

If you were around in the 1980s, then you know that the invention of the cordless phone occurred during this time. No longer were we confined to that ten-foot cord on the kitchen phone. We could actually walk around the house! Of course, the phone was so heavy we could only walk so far before needing to sit and rest, but I digress…

The 1980s was also the decade of big hair. Desiring to look their best, ladies went through hairspray by the caseload, thus creating a hole in the ozone layer.

Hairspray, I might add, is also central to one of my most enduring high school memories. A big-haired young lady got too friendly with a Bunsen burner and…SCHWOOP! In about 1.4 seconds, her hair plumed into a smoky fireball, sending the singed girl to the nurse and the class into hysterics. But, again, I digress…

Finally, the 1980s was the decade when the boy band New Kids on the Block commanded the airwaves. Now, why do I risk horrific flashbacks to bring them up, you ask? Well, my sister, Stephanie, worshipped this boy band.

Stephanie bought every album and cassette tape (remember those?) that this group produced. If NKOTB put it out, she bought it. I could sing the song, "Hangin' Tough"—which I hated—because I heard it five thousand times. You may think I'm exaggerating, but I'm serious. Five thousand times!

She had NKOTB t-shirts, hats, jackets, socks, etc. If there was an article of clothing with their faces on it, my sister had it! She had NKOTB bed sheets, pillowcases, and comforter. It wasn't just enough to listen to them all day, Stephanie had to be clothed in them and then sleep with them knitted into her sheets. I mean, come on!

As if all that wasn't bad enough, she woke up with them too. Cereal! NKOTB cereal? Whaaaaat? And did I mention she had all their dolls as well as a plastic music stage on which to set them up? Because she did.

You can imagine that when she was old enough to attend one of their concerts, she was literally beside herself. Stephanie and a friend even paid a ton extra for a "backstage experience"…one that I still hear about to this day!

CONSIDER

Maybe you've had the chance to visit your favorite team during pre-season workouts, scored backstage passes to a concert involving your favorite band, or had a chance encounter with a well-known celebrity. Each opportunity opens up the chance to potentially get an autograph or a selfie, as well as a story you will tell over and over again.

In our Scripture for today, a few Greek men wanted such an opportunity with Jesus—get a quick meet and greet so they could tell everyone, "Hey, I met Jesus, and we hung out!" Jesus, however, does not allow for such things. There is no simply "meeting Jesus." You are either all in or all out.

As you read, consider if you sometimes treat Jesus as a celebrity you can meet from time to time, or as your Lord who demands total devotion.

READ: JOHN 12

INVEST

Contrast Mary's devotion to Jesus with Judas's desire to use Jesus for material gain:

What do verses 10-11 say about the Pharisees and other leaders?

Surrendering to Jesus would have cost the religious leaders their positions and their influence. What might be holding you back from complete surrender?

In verses 23-26, what did Jesus say when Philip and Andrew told Him that some folks wanted a "meet and greet"?

Would you say you have died to self? Why or why not?

Would you say that you "care nothing for life in this world" (verse 25)? Why or why not?

Why did many refuse to surrender to Jesus according to verses 42-43?

How does fear of losing things, coupled with a desire to be recognized, affect your decision to surrender fully to Christ?

PRAY

- Thank Jesus for being the Savior of the world
- Confess, if necessary, refusing to surrender fully to the Lord
- Ask the Lord to help you die to self that you might live for Him
- Ask the Lord to strengthen you to seek after His praise and not the world's praise

TRAINING

- Spend some time examining your life. Isolate the things that you have difficulty surrendering
- What is holding you back from complete surrender? A lack of trust God will provide, a desire to build a career, a family? Seek to understand the root of any "unsurrendered" portions of your life
- Hand those things over to the Lord one by one

JOHN 13

START HERE
If you love something, set it free.
If it comes back, it was, and always will be, yours.
If it never returns, it was never yours to begin with.
If it just sits in your living room,
messes up your stuff,
eats all your food,
is constantly using a phone,
takes your money,
and never behaves,
it's probably one of your kids.

CONSIDER
Love is an action verb. Saying, "I love you" is an easy thing. Showing "I love you," well, that takes more work. In John 13, Jesus puts love on display and challenges His disciples to mirror that display. For, as Jesus says, it is by our love that people will know we are His disciples (verse 35).

As you read, consider how well you "show love" in your everyday life.

READ: JOHN 13

INVEST
In Bible times, it was the job of the lowest slave to wash the feet of those entering the house. The lowest slave was issued this chore because the dirt roads of the day—filled with animal urine and feces—would have left sandaled feet caked in grime and filth. How does knowing this make Jesus' act in verses 3-5 more significant?

According to verses 12-15, why did Jesus wash His disciples' feet?

How well are you following Jesus' example of selfless service? Where could you improve?

What does Jesus say in verses 34-35?

Can people tell you are a disciple of Jesus by how you love others? Why or why not?

What can you do to serve someone selflessly this week?

What can you do to display Christ's love to someone this week?

Who can help you follow through on these things this week?

PRAY
- Thank Jesus for His tremendous example of selfless love
- Confess, if necessary, not following that example
- Ask the Lord to fill you with His love that it might spill out of you into others
- Ask the Lord to provide you with opportunities to love and serve others this week

TRAINING
- Don't move on from this devotion until you have answered the final three questions in the INVEST section
- Be alert for opportunities to love and serve others this week

JOHN 14

START HERE

A father had won a toy at an office party. He called his three kids together to ask which one should have the present. "Who is the most obedient?" he asked.

The children all stared back at him in silence. Then he asked a second question. "Who never talks back to mother?"

Again, the kids appeared to be mystified by the question.

Finally, Dad asked, "Who does everything Mommy says?"

With that question, the kids were finally able to come to a conclusion. The three small voices answered in unison, "Okay, Dad, you get the toy."[63]

Children, of course, are called to love and obey their parents. As children of God, it is no different. We are to love and obey our Heavenly Father.

CONSIDER

In John 14:6, Jesus famously states, *"I am the way, the truth, and the life. No one can come to Father except through me."* From this, we know that only through Jesus can we experience eternity in Heaven.

Knowing this, the question becomes, "How do we connect with Jesus?" The Lord Himself gives the answer: Trust and obey. We trust that Jesus is the Son of God who paid the penalty for our sins, and we show our love and devotion through obedience.

As you read, consider how deeply you know the truth, and how well you obey the Lord.

READ: JOHN 14

INVEST

How do we see Jesus' love for us in verses 18-20?

As we discussed yesterday, love is an action verb. We see Jesus displaying such love through His love and obedience to the Father. How are we to display love according to verses 15, 21, 23, and 24?

Why do you think Jesus repeats these things four times in nine verses (and adds a fifth involving Himself in verse 31)?

If someone secretly filmed your life over the past seven days, could people watch and tell you are living a life of obedience to God?

What has been going well? What areas need work?

Today, in our culture, many want to pick and choose which Scriptures to believe and to obey. Why is this *not* an option?

Obedience is only truly seen when we don't like something, yet obey nonetheless. We will obey if we enjoy it. "Have ice cream for dinner." Okay, I will obey! "Deny yourself, pick up your cross, and follow." Um, I think I'll pass. How about you? Do you strive to obey the whole counsel of God, or do you tend to pick and choose based on personal preference and cultural trends?

PRAY
- Thank the Lord for being the way, the truth, and the life
- Confess, if necessary, not fully trusting and/or not fully obeying
- Ask the Lord to deepen your trust in Him
- Ask the Lord to fill you with a desire to obey *everything* that is in His Word

TRAINING
Examine your level of obedience in the following areas:
- The whole of God's Word
- Your actions
- Your attitudes

- Your words
- Your thoughts
- Your choices
- Your relationships

What areas need some work? Give those areas to the Lord and begin anew.

JOHN 15

START HERE

Mr. Smythe had been giving his second-grade students a short lesson on science. He had explained about magnets and showed how they would pick up nails, pennies, and other metallic objects. Now it was question time. "Class," he began, "My name begins with the letter 'M,' and I can pick up things around the house. What am I?"

A little boy in the front row shot up his hand. "Yes, Billy. What am I?"

"You're a mother!"[64]

Magnets are fascinating objects. They can either repel things or draw them near depending on which pole is at work. Two magnets with the same poles facing each other will refuse to draw near, while opposite poles will create quite a strong bond.

In our relationship with God, we can be much like magnets. We can either draw close to the Lord or push Him away. It's up to us each day to decide which pole we will offer.

CONSIDER

The Greek word *meno* is used ten times in the first ten verses of John 15. It means to *remain, abide,* or *be continuously present.* In other words, stay connected. This is Jesus' command to us. As a sheep must *meno* with the shepherd for safety, and a grape must *meno* with the vine for nutrients and growth, so we must *meno* with the Lord.

When we do so, there is life and victory. When we do not, there is shriveling and loss. As you read, consider what you are doing each day to remain, abide, and be continuously present with the Lord.

READ: JOHN 15

INVEST

What is Jesus saying in verses 4-8?

In chapter 14, Jesus intimately connected love with obedience *five* times. Why do you think He does this two more times in chapter 15? (See verses 10 and 14.)

How will obedience help keep you connected to the Savior?

How does disobedience work to disconnect you from Him?

In verses 12 and 17, Jesus reminds His disciples (and us) of a command He gave in chapter 13. What is it?

Loving God, through obedience, is just part of what is necessary to stay connected to the Savior. The other part is loving those around you and not allowing Satan to cause division through anger, bitterness, resentment, and more. Where might you need some help to better love others?

What can you do this week to put love on display for others to see?

PRAY
- Thank Jesus for being the Vine on which you can grow
- Confess, if necessary, not *meno*-ing with Jesus as you should
- Ask the Lord to help you remain, abide, and be continuously present with Him
- Ask the Lord to use you to love others this week

TRAINING
A grape is going nowhere without the vine. Once disconnected from the vine, it will shrivel and die. Connected, it will be nourished and grow. Likewise, in our relationship with the Lord, we must have the same mindset. We have nothing apart from Christ. Apart from Him we will shrivel and die spiritually. Connected, we will be nourished and grow.

We need Him every moment. He must be our source and our all. If you do not view Jesus in this manner, spend some time in prayer

JOHN 16

START HERE

There's a story of a man who sought the perfect picture of peace. Not finding one that satisfied, he announced a contest to produce this masterpiece. The challenge stirred the imagination of artists everywhere, and paintings arrived from far and wide.

Finally, the great day arrived. The judges uncovered one peaceful scene after another, while the viewers clapped and cheered. At last, only two pictures remained veiled. As a judge pulled the cover from one, a hush fell over the crowd. A mirror-smooth lake reflected lacy, green birches under the soft blush of the evening sky. Along the grassy shore, a flock of sheep grazed undisturbed. Surely this was the winner.

The man with the vision uncovered the second painting himself, and the crowd gasped in surprise. Could this be peace? A tumultuous waterfall cascaded down a rocky precipice; those gathered could almost feel the cold, penetrating spray. Dark, steel-gray clouds threatened to explode with lightning, wind, and rain. In the midst of the thundering noises and bitter chill, a spindly tree clung to the rocks at the edge of the falls. One of its branches reached out in front of the torrential waters as if foolishly seeking to experience its full power.

Tucked in the elbow of that branch, a little bird had built a nest. And, in that nest, rested three small chicks content and undisturbed in their stormy surroundings. How was that possible? It was possible because their mother, with wings outstretched, protected them from all earthly turmoil.

Is this peace? Yes, and it is the same kind of peace that Jesus gives. For peace is not the absence of conflict, but the knowledge that you are safe and secure regardless of what surrounds you.

CONSIDER

John 16 ends with some of Jesus' most comforting words, *"Here on earth you will have trials and sorrows. But take heart, because I have overcome the world"* (verse 33).

The fact that there *will* be trials and sorrows here on earth is undeniable. But, equally undeniable, is the fact that we are not alone. We have a Savior, and that Savior promised us the Holy Spirit. More than that, through Christ's sacrifice on our behalf, He opened a way to the Father. All of God's power, grace, guidance, wisdom, and love is just a prayer away.

As you read, consider how you are living your life—like you are all alone or like you have the Father, Son, and Holy Spirit by your side.

READ: JOHN 16

INVEST
According to verse 7, who is available to us because of Jesus' death?

What will the Spirit do for us according to verses 8-14?

Do you seek the Spirit's wisdom and guidance, and do you allow Him to convict you of sin and direct you toward righteousness?

Where are you doing well? What needs some work?

In verses 23-24, Jesus talks about praying in His name. Some think that this simply means tacking Jesus' name to the end of every prayer and then God is obliged to answer. This is not the case. Names in Bible times were far more than mere monikers. They were representative of people's character. So, to pray in Jesus' name is to pray according to who He is. With this in mind, how does this knowledge potentially change your understanding of praying in Jesus' name?

How good is it to know that you are not alone in this world?

Where do you need the Father, Son, and Holy Spirit to work in your life or in the lives of those around you?

PRAY
- Thank Jesus for the peace you can have knowing that Christ has

already overcome

- Confess, if necessary, living life more like you are alone than like you have the Trinity at your side
- Ask the Lord to fill you with His peace and strength
- Ask the Lord to work in your life and in the lives of those around you

TRAINING

Some gifts never get used—like fruitcake. Here's my theory on fruitcake. There is really only one fruitcake in the world, and it just keeps getting passed off from person to person.

But anyway, let's not treat God's gift of peace like a fruitcake. The next trial comes along, and you start worrying again instead of using the gift. Somebody cuts you off on the freeway, and you start getting frustrated again instead of grabbing hold of peace. When trials come, you must pray and focus on the Lord so that His peace can work in you.

Think about what you've been through the last week or two. Have you had any troubles, any trials, any struggles? Have you seen peace come and go with circumstances and people? If so, are you ready to receive God's gift of peace that never ends?

If you're tempted to doubt that such a gift exists, I challenge you to:
- Pray for the gift of peace. Say, "Lord, I hear you have a peace that is hard for me to imagine, and I need that peace. My life has problems, struggles, and issues, and the peace I have never lasts. Please, Lord, give me Your peace. A peace that surpasses all understanding and never ends."
- Open the gift the of peace. You must open a gift for it to become yours. It's one thing to say the words and ask God for His peace; it's another thing to actually grab hold of it
- Use the gift of peace. Focus on this gift that you have. Feel God's arms spread out over you as you travel through whatever trial you are going through

JOHN 17

START HERE

Dwight L. Moody once stated, "A holy life will make the deepest impression. Lighthouses blow no horns, they just shine."

Our connection with Christ should develop a radiant faith that turns heads much like a person wearing neon clothes or having brightly dyed hair causes a double take. For instance, when my wife, son, and I went to the Great Wolf Lodge (a hotel with a large indoor waterpark) one time, we quickly noticed a young woman with bright (and I mean bright) pink hair.

You couldn't help but notice—in a sea of blondes, brunettes, and redheads, that pink hair stood out! Really stood out! Likewise, those around us should not be able to help but take notice of Christ in us—His love, His grace, His holiness, and His truth. Even when surrounded by a sea of people, we should "stick out."

CONSIDER

In Jesus' heartfelt prayer from this chapter, our Savior expertly weaves three main themes. Seven times He uses the word *glory,* six times the words *one* or *united,* and six times the words *message, truth,* or *Word.* Through this, we will see that God is most glorified as we live out His truth while living in harmony with His people.

As you read, consider if your life is marked by giving glory to God in those ways.

READ: JOHN 17

INVEST

The Greek word most often translated *glory* in the New Testament (one hundred and fifty times) means "brightness" or "shining." In other words, bringing glory to God is like shining a spotlight on who He is. Would you say that you are living in a way that shines a light on what God is really like?

One way to help ensure that you are giving God glory is to live by His Word.

What do verses 6, 8, and 17 say about this?

When believers fight, argue, gossip, and backbite, it shines an unflattering light, making the Lord look bad. This is why Jesus prayed for unity. What does He pray specifically in verses 11 and 21-23?

Are you living in unity with your fellow believers?

How can you be a force for unity in your church?

In verse 14, Jesus states that the world will hate His people because of their adherence to His Word and His truth. If you find your views on same-sex marriage, abortion, entertainment standards, and how to get to Heaven meet with little to no resistance, what might that tell you about your stance on His truth?

In verses 3-4, Jesus gives us the path to follow—come to God through Christ alone, live out faith in Him, shining a glorious spotlight on God, then enter into that glory through our death. Is this the path you are currently following?

What might need to change?

PRAY
- Thank God for the opportunities He gives you to bring glory to His name
- Confess, if necessary, not shining a true spotlight on who the Lord really is
- Ask the Lord to use you to bring glory to His name
- Ask the Lord to enable you to be a force for unity in your church

TRAINING
- Ask yourself some questions: Will I live for my own goals, comfort, and pleasure; or will I live for Christ and His glory? How might my

priorities need to be adjusted?

- Evaluate how you have been spending your time over the last few weeks. Understand that if Jesus is the reason for everything, you cannot be content with free time spent solely for self
- Continually remind yourself that this world is not your home and that everything in the world that you hold so dear will not last
- Consider how you are reflecting Christ. Is the reflection pointed straight back at yourself or are you shining outwardly for Christ?
- Consider how much of your life is surrendered to the Lord. Is it one hundred percent? If not, what parts have not been surrendered yet?

JOHN 18

START HERE
How can you tell if you are a fair weather fan? Well, here are a few indicators:

- If you have sprained more than one ankle jumping from one bandwagon to another, you just may be a fair weather fan
- If all your favorite teams happen to be the winningest teams in sports' history, you just may be a fair weather fan
- If you can't name half the players on your favorite team, you just may be a fair weather fan
- If a team is your favorite because you like its colors, you just may be a fair weather fan
- If your favorite player changes every year, you just may be a fair weather fan
- If you let your fantasy team determine your favorite team, you just may be a fair weather fan
- If you have never even been to the city where your favorite team is located, you just may be a fair weather fan
- If you have never experienced a losing season in your life, you just may be a fair weather fan
- If you root for "whoever Lebron plays for," you ARE a fair weather fan

If you are a fair weather fan with sports, then so be it. However, let's all strive never to be fair weather fans with the Lord.

CONSIDER
During the Last Supper, while sitting in a cozy upper room, Peter affirms to Jesus, "I am ready to die for you" (John 13:37).

It is easy, when all seems right with the world, to claim love and faithfulness. However, when the world gets turned upside down, that's when love and faithfulness truly get tested. During difficult times, some (like Judas) will reject Jesus out of hand. Others are more like Peter. There's a strong desire to follow Christ on the good days, but when things get rough…

As you read, consider if you are a fair weather Christian or if you are all in.

READ: JOHN 18

INVEST

How do we see an open betrayal of Jesus in verses 1-3?

Peter experiences the power of Jesus' words literally knock soldiers backward. Seeing this, how does the big fisherman react in verse 10?

After the authorities arrest Jesus (who now seems weak), how does Peter respond in verses 15-27?

Do you tend to be a little like Peter? In with Jesus when everything is good but doubting, complaining, and lacking faith when things aren't so good?

If you answered "yes," what can you do about this?

What is Pilate's famous line to Jesus in verse 38?

If Pilate had known truth, his life would have been much different. (History tells us that he eventually committed suicide.) Knowing the truth about Jesus changes everything, so how can continually reminding yourself of the truth about Jesus—He is Savior, powerful, loving, faithful—help you when difficult times come?

PRAY
- Thank Jesus for His willingness to die for a world that often denies and rejects Him
- Confess, if necessary, being a fair weather Christian
- Ask the Lord to continually remind you of His love, faithfulness, power, and sacrifice on your behalf
- Ask the Lord to heighten your understanding of His Word and His truth

TRAINING

- Check out "Worldview University" at providencefoundation.com/home/worldview-university/
- Understanding God's truth in today's relativistic age is vital. Don't miss what you could learn from studying a biblical worldview

JOHN 19

START HERE

The Roman legionnaire steps forward with the flagrum (or flagellum) in his hand. This is a short whip consisting of several heavy, leather thongs with two small balls of lead attached near the ends of each. The heavy whip is brought down with full force again and again across Jesus' shoulders, back, and legs.

At first, the thongs cut through the skin only. Then, as the blows continue, they cut deeper into the subcutaneous tissues, producing first an oozing of blood from the capillaries and veins of the skin, and finally spurting arterial bleeding from vessels in the underlying muscles. The small balls of lead first produce large, deep bruises which are broken open by subsequent blows. Finally, the skin of the back is hanging in long ribbons and the entire area is an unrecognizable mass of torn, bleeding tissue. When it is determined by the centurion in charge that the prisoner is near death, the beating is finally stopped. The half-fainting Jesus is then untied and allowed to slump to the stone pavement, wet with His own blood.

Later, when Jesus finally makes it to the site of the crucifixion, he is quickly thrown backward with His shoulders against the wood. The legionnaire feels for the depression at the front of the wrist. He drives a heavy, square, wrought-iron nail through the wrist and deep into the wood. Quickly, he moves to the other side and repeats the action, being careful not to pull the arms too tightly, but to allow some flex and movement...

The left foot is now pressed backward against the right foot, and with both feet extended, toes down, a nail is driven through the arch of each, leaving the knees moderately flexed. The victim is now crucified. As He slowly sags down with more weight on the nails in the wrists, excruciating pain shoots along the fingers and up the arms to explode in the brain — the nails in the wrists are putting pressure on the median nerves.

As He pushes Himself upward to avoid this stretching torment, He places His full weight on the nail through His feet. Again, there is the searing agony of the nail tearing through the nerves between the metatarsal bones of the feet. At this point, as the arms fatigue, great waves of cramps sweep over the muscles, knotting them in deep, relentless, throbbing pain. With these cramps comes the inability to push Himself upward. Hanging by his arms, the pectoral muscles are paralyzed and the intercostal muscles are unable to act. Air can be drawn into the lungs but cannot be exhaled. Jesus fights to raise Himself in order to get even one short breath. Finally, carbon dioxide builds up in the lungs and in the blood stream and the cramps partially subside. Spasmodically, he is able to push Himself upward to exhale and bring in the life-giving oxygen...

Jesus experiences hours of limitless pain, cycles of twisting, joint-rending cramps, intermittent partial asphyxiation, searing pain where tissue is torn from His lacerated back as He moves up and down against the rough timber. Then another agony begins -- a terrible crushing pain deep in the chest as the pericardium slowly fills with serum and begins to compress the heart. One remembers again the 22nd Psalm, the 14th verse: "I am poured out like water, and all my bones are out of joint; my heart is like wax; it is melted in the midst of my bowels."

It is now almost over. The loss of tissue fluids has reached a critical level; the compressed heart is struggling to pump heavy, thick, sluggish blood into the tissue; the tortured lungs are making a frantic effort to gasp in small gulps of air. The markedly dehydrated tissues send their flood of stimuli to the brain. Jesus gasps His fifth cry, "I thirst."

The body of Jesus is now in extremes, and He can feel the chill of death creeping through His tissues. This realization brings out His sixth words, possibly little more than a tortured whisper, "It is finished." His mission of atonement has completed. Finally, He can allow His body to die. With one last surge of strength, he once again presses His torn feet against the nail, straightens His legs, takes a deeper breath, and utters His seventh and last cry, "Father! Into thy hands, I commit My spirit."[65]

CONSIDER

The most monumental event in history began on a Friday morning long ago. Jesus would head to the cross to die for the world He created. Yet, just a few days later, He would burst forth from the tomb, providing victory for all who would believe.

As you read, consider if you have truly embraced how life-changing the cross and the empty tomb are.

READ: JOHN 19

INVEST

What did Jesus ensure for you in verses 1-3 and 18?

During this event, Pilate was only interested in keeping the peace and protecting his position. Have you been guilty of not sharing your faith because you don't want to upset anyone or lose "status points" with friends, family, coworkers, etc.?

In verse 30, Jesus utters, "It is finished." In the Greek, He states, "Teleos," which literally means "paid in full." This word was often stamped on bills when they were paid off. Why is it significant that Jesus chose to use this word at the end?

What did Joseph and Nicodemus do for Jesus in verses 38-42?

Handling a bloody, dead body would have made both men unfit for Sabbath worship. This meant that Joseph and Nicodemus would not have been permitted to enter the Temple on the special Passover Sabbath. These men gave up much for Jesus' sake. How does this contrast greatly with Pilate?

Would you say that you are more like Pilate or more like Joseph and Nicodemus?

What can you do this week to stand up for Jesus and share the Gospel?

PRAY
- Thank Jesus for the cross and the empty tomb
- Confess, if necessary, being more like Pilate than Joseph and Nicodemus
- Ask the Lord to provide you opportunities to serve Him this week
- Ask the Lord to mold you into a willing and able servant

TRAINING

- Keeping praying for the five people on your prayer card and seek opportunities to share the Gospel with at least one of them this week
- Review what Jesus endured on the cross. Let His willingness to suffer on your behalf encourage you to stand for Him

JOHN 20

START HERE

There's a funny little cartoon strip with "Doubting Thomas" complaining to his fellow disciples. His robed arms stretched high in exasperation, he states, "All I'm saying is that we don't call Peter 'Denying Peter' or Mark 'Ran away naked Mark,' so why do I have to be saddled with this title?!?"[66]

Yes, I think Thomas has gotten a pretty bad wrap. After all, when it comes to doubting what God can do, are we really any better?

CONSIDER

When Jesus miraculously rose from the dead, He defeated Satan, sin, and the grave! Absolutely amazing and totally incredible! Only, His closest followers didn't even believe it really happened.

It is not uncommon to get the same reaction today. An unbelieving world calling miraculous healings luck, perfectly timed events called coincidences, changed lives labeled self-help, and more. Sadly, even among Christians, there is doubt.

As you read, consider how often the Lord has proved Himself in your life.

READ: JOHN 20

INVEST

Who did Mary think Jesus was in verse 15?

In verses 24-25, how does Thomas react to the news of Jesus' resurrection?

According to verse 31, what was John's purpose in writing this Gospel?

Do you tend to have doubts about whether or not Jesus wants to answer your prayers and work in your life?

What can help diminish these doubts and worries?

As you made your way through the four gospels, how can reminding yourself of all that you have read help keep you at peace, knowing that Jesus is working for your good?

PRAY
- Thank Jesus for all of His answers to prayer in your life
- Confess, if necessary, any doubts or worries you may have about the love, faithfulness, and goodness of God
- Ask the Lord to recall the many blessings He has bestowed upon your life
- Ask the Lord to fill you with peace, love, joy, and hope

TRAINING
- By yourself, or with your family, come up with something you can thank God for using every letter of the alphabet

JOHN 21

START HERE

Brad Walden, senior minister with the Tate's Creek Christian Church, in Lexington, Kentucky, tells a true story about a nine year-old named Mark. One day Mark's mother received a phone call in the middle of the afternoon. It was a teacher from her son's school.

"Mrs. Smith," the teacher started, "something unusual happened today in your son's class. Your son did something that surprised me so much that I thought you should know about it immediately."

The mother, of course, began to worry. *Oh dear, what in the world did my son do?* She thought to herself.

The teacher continued, "Nothing like this has happened in all my years of teaching. This morning I was teaching a lesson on creative writing. And, as I always do, I tell the story of the ant and the grasshopper: The ant works hard all summer and stores up plenty of food, but the grasshopper plays all summer and does not work. Then winter comes. The grasshopper begins to starve because he has no food. So, he begins to beg, 'Please, Mr. Ant, you have so much food. Please, let me eat, too.'"

"Then I finished by saying, 'All right, boys and girls, your job is to write the ending to the story.' Well, your son asked if he could draw a picture, and I told him that he could so long as he first wrote an ending to the story."

"As in all the years past, some of the students said the ant shared his food through the winter, and both the ant and the grasshopper lived, while some other children write, 'No, Mr. Grasshopper. You should have worked in the summer. Now, I have just enough food for myself.' So, the ant lived, and the grasshopper died.'"

"But your son ended the story in a way different from any other child I've ever taught. He wrote, 'So the ant gave all of his food to the grasshopper; the grasshopper lived through the winter. But the ant died.' And the picture? At the bottom of the page, Mark had drawn three crosses."

Like that grasshopper, we've done our own thing and neglected what we should have been doing and how we should have been living. We sinned. And in our fall from grace, we removed ourselves from a relationship with God.

Worse, there was no way for us to get back into that relationship, for we cannot save ourselves.

But Jesus' love for us was so great that He willingly gave up His all for us. He died so that we could live.

CONSIDER
The Gospels end with a call on Peter's life to make a Kingdom difference in the world, to forsake self, and to follow Christ no matter the consequence. Peter, of course, would go on to do just that. However, as we finish up the book of John, he is less than enthusiastic about it!

Three times Jesus will ask Peter if he loves Him. The first time, the Lord uses the Greek word *agape*—which is self-sacrificing, unconditional love. In essence, Jesus says, "Will you sacrifice unconditionally out of love for me more than the rest of these?"

Peter responds using the Greek word *phileo*—which means brotherly or friendship love—in essence replying, "Lord, you know I am your friend." Not exactly what Jesus was looking for! So, He brings it down a notch. Dropping "more than the rest of these," Jesus simply asks, "Will you sacrifice unconditionally out of love for me?"

Again, Peter responds with *phileo*. "You know I am Your friend."

A third time, Jesus will ask Peter a question. Only this time, He will drop down to *phileo* and ask, "Are you my friend?" In this, we see the Lord's willingness to meet Peter where he is in order to bring him up to where he needs to be.

As you read, consider where you are spiritually. How far from sacrificial and unconditional love are you in your relationship with Jesus?

READ: JOHN 21

INVEST
The Lord provides a plentiful catch of fish for a group of men who recently denied and abandoned Him. What does that tell you about Jesus?

How does this encourage you during the times you come up short?

How often have you seen Jesus bend down to your level in order to pick you up?

How can you praise the Lord for this?

Who can you help raise up?

PRAY
- Thank Jesus for His sacrificial and unconditional love for you
- Confess, if necessary, not reciprocating that kind of love
- Ask the Lord to fill you with His *agape* love
- Ask the Lord to let His *agape* love spill out of you into others

TRAINING
- Don't let the end of this devotional keep you from meeting daily with the Lord
- Consider grabbing a copy of my *Letters of Paul* devotional or *The First 100 Days of the Rest of Your Life*

EPILOGUE

You made it to the end! Congratulations!

I hope God has truly blessed you during this journey through the Gospels. I know He deeply desires to do so many awesome things in and through you. His plan for your life is truly remarkable! I trust you will grab hold of that.

If you have been blessed in any way through this devotional, I'd love to hear about it. Feel free to contact me through www.markjmusser.com.

APPENDIX

1. http://jokes.christiansunite.com/Christmas/Jesus_is_Better_Than_Santa.shtml
2. https://www.reddit.com/r/Jokes/comments/40vbui/repentance/
3. 2 Timothy 2:21
4. http://www.cityharvestagchurch.org/joke-on-temptation/
5. https://corechristianity.com/resource-library/articles/7-ways-to-resist-temptation
6. http://javacasa.com/humor/sermon.htm
7. http://www.cityharvestagchurch.org/jokes-on-faith/
8. http://saltforsermons.org.uk/category/evangelism/
9. www.laughnet.net/archive/misc/insuranc.htm
10. Idleman, Kyle *Not a Fan: Becoming a Completely Committed Follower of Jesus,* Zondervan, 2011
11. http://www.kentcrockett.com/cgi-bin/illustrations/index.cgi?topic=Judging
12. http://www.positivelypresent.com/2009/05/stop-judging.html
13. https://www.foxnews.com/lifestyle/bridezilla-secretly-fattens-up-her-sister-bridesmaids-before-wedding-to-be-center-of-attention
14. http://www.sermonillustrations.com/a-z/s/self_centered.htm
15. https://www.mayoclinic.org/healthy-lifestyle/adult-health/in-depth/forgiveness/art-20047692
16. http://www.sermonillustrations.com/a-z/p/priorities.htm
17. https://bible.org/illustration/besetting-sin
18. Campbell, Donald *Daniel, Decoder of Dreams*, Victor 1979
19. *Today in the Word*, April 3, 1992
20. https://byebyeboringday.wordpress.com/school-time/99-fun-things-to-do-in-a-boring-lesson/
21. http://www.sermonillustrations.com/a-z/s/second_coming.htm
22. https://www.backyardchickens.com/threads/the-bricklayers-insurance-claim.385709/
23. https://www.sunnyskyz.com/feel-good-story/2766/At-The-Crossroads
24. "My Victory" 2016 SixSteps Music, Capitalpublishing.com David Crowder, Ed Cash, Hank Bentley and Darren Mulligan
25. https://www.insight.org/resources/bible/the-gospels/mark
26. IBID
27. https://jaymccarl.com/2016/07/25/the-one-word-telegram/
28. North, Jessica Nelson, "The Tea Party"

29. Lieghton Ford, Good News is for Sharing, 1977, David C. Cook Publishing Co.

30. https://www.cru.org/us/en/train-and-grow/spiritual-growth/prayer/pray-for-persecuted-church.html

31. http://www.jokes4us.com/peoplejokes/farmerjokes.html

32. 2 Corinthians 2:11

33. https://www.ministry127.com/resources/illustration/humility-demonstrated

34. Today in the Word, June 11, 1992

35. http://corsinet.com/braincandy/hlife2.html

36. https://www.insight.org/resources/bible/the-gospels/luke

37. IBID

38. http://www.sermonillustrations.com/a-z/t/thanksgiving.htm

39. Slaughter, Mike *Christmas is Not Your Birthday: Experience the Joy of Living and Giving Like Jesus* Abington Press, 2011

40. Luke 1:78b,79a

41. https://maxlucado.com/a-christmas-prayer/

42. https://www.navigators.org/resource/how-to-memorize-scripture/

43. https://www.dailydot.com/irl/girlfriends-rules-emotional-abuse/

44. https://bible.org/seriespage/2-process-spirituality-being-versus-doing

45. Wycliffe Handbook of Preaching & Preachers, Moody, 1984

46. http://www.lawrencewilson.com/how-to-be-humble/

47. https://unlockingthebible.org/2016/07/10-questions-for-examining-your-life/

48. https://storiesforpreaching.com/category/sermonillustrations/humility/

49. https://www.phrases.org.uk/meanings/there-but-for-the-grace-of-god.html

50. https://en.wikipedia.org/wiki/John_Bradford

51. http://www.ebaumsworld.com/jokes/hide-and-seek/5322/

52. https://thoughtcatalog.com/nico-lang/2013/09/moist-and-28-other-gross-sounding-english-words-that-everyone-hates/4/

53. Wilde, Oscar *De Profundis* Digireads.com 2011

54. http://www.sermonillustrations.com/a-z/a/appearances.htm

55. Pile, Stephen *The Ultimate Book of Heroic Failures* Faber and Faber, 2012

56. https://www.insight.org/resources/bible/the-gospels/john

57. IBID

58. http://saltforsermons.org.uk/category/gods-love/

59. http://jokes.christiansunite.com/Amish/A_Miracle_Transformation.shtml

60. https://www.joniandfriends.org/jonis-corner/jonis-bio/

61. http://www.jokes4us.com/animaljokes/sheepjokes.html
62. http://saltforsermons.org.uk/category/death/
63. http://www.cityharvestagchurch.org/obey-your-parents-joke/
64. http://www.jokebuddha.com/Magnet#ixzz5WkaEqCWp
65. http://www1.cbn.com/medical-view-of-the-crucifixion-of-jesus-christ
66. Harris, Joshua 2010

Made in the USA
Monee, IL
20 September 2022

14288427R00155